The Creative Cook

The Creative Cook

The secrets of the kitchen revealed

James Kempston

Weidenfeld & Nicolson, London

Text copyright
© James Kempston 1993

First published in Great
Britain in 1993 by George
Weidenfeld and Nicolson
Ltd, Orion House, 5 Upper
St Martin's Lane, London
WC2H 9EA

Designed by Atelier
Illustrated by Mette Heinz

*British Library Cataloguing-
in-Publication Data*
A catalogue record for this
book is available from the
British Library.

ISBN 0–297–83022–8

Typeset by Selwood Systems,
Midsomer Norton
Printed and bound in Great
Britain by Butler & Tanner Ltd

Acknowledgements

In putting this book together, I'm indebted to
Ethne Clarke for making me an offer I couldn't
refuse and to Vicky Hayward, whose knowledgeable advice made a cogent whole from a
series of random jottings. My thanks also to
the editorial team at Weidenfeld and Nicolson
for their unfailing help and patience and to
Harold McGee for providing a scientific base
for my culinary intuitions. All this help would
be as nothing without the help of Ingrid, who,
with love and care, made room in our relation-
ship for this major intrusion.

Contents

Introduction

As a child, I always thought it was a better idea to sit by the kitchen range, and run the risk of having to peel the potatoes, than go outside to play in the frosty morning – 'getting a bit of fresh air' as it was called – and get thoroughly chilled in the process. It meant being warm, being close to the cooking of food (of which I was bound to get a mouthful or two) and being safe; it is easy to see how I came to think of the kitchen as a good place to be in.

It wasn't long before potato peeling lost its charm and it was time to move onto the creative side of the kitchen and make good tastes of my own. The first attempt that I remember – I was eight at the time – was trying to combine my two favourite tastes of the moment into one tasting twice as good. As these two tastes were peppermint rock and crisp bacon, the experiment ended in smoky disaster and earned me a hiding hard enough to fix the experiment in my mind forever. Later experiments, forced by a wartime ration of a miserly two ounces of sweets per week, involved combining honey, margarine and powdered milk to make a chewy confection vaguely like toffee and compelling enough to have me race home after school, dash into the kitchen and get it made and consumed before it was cold. Hardly a promising beginning.

The privations of wartime rationing did have one beneficial effect however. Making good food by strictly following a recipe was almost impossible then, since rarely were all the specified ingredients to hand at the same time. Intelligent substitution became the order of the day. (I remember one bizarre substitution was to exchange the cooking fat needed in shortcrust pastry for liquid paraffin. This worked surprisingly well until the local chemist, alarmed at the run on his liquid paraffin stocks, started to flavour it with peppermint.) This soon taught me how to make food which was somewhere near a recipe's intention but included several different ingredients – a good grounding for making tasty food without a recipe at all.

It is the aim of this book to pass on that basic approach and show how to read a recipe thinking of it as an inspirational springboard not as a set of instructions and ingredients. Some of the recipes have been expanded in certain areas to illustrate how this creative process could work. I've chosen generally well known dishes for this purpose, since the thinking behind them should become clearer if the taste of the end result is known already. Other recipes have been chosen either because they are the ones I'm using currently, and are therefore fresh and zingy to me, or because they seem particularly good at illustrating a point – like the affinity between soufflés and sponges.

1 Palate Awareness

If forced to say why food is good, many of us find it difficult to get beyond words like 'delicious', 'tasty' or 'scrumptious'. If pressed further, we might become more specific and use words like 'succulent', 'tender' or 'juicy' and we might just mention the novelty of the taste or how pretty it looks. Few would refer to colours or colour contrasts, mouth effects, or variations in temperature. Yet all of these factors play a part in giving food enough presence to be thought of as being good to eat. Those cooks who rely on recipes to achieve this desirable quality will need to become aware of these factors, and the senses they involve, if they are to explore the uncharted world of creating their own good food.

Food passing through the mouth is screened for being good to eat or not. The senses that do this screening react to the taste, texture, look and smell of food and send signals to the brain as to whether it is alright to eat. These signals are strong at first but they weaken with successive mouthfuls of the same food which has the same stimulants. Anyone who has smelt a rose repeatedly will know this effect. But when food containing a variety of different but pleasant stimulants continues to arrive, a stream of strong messages goes to the brain emphasizing the 'good taste' of the food, and continues to do so until such time as the senses are completely satiated.

The enjoyment of food does not, however, just depend on the stimulants the food contains or even on the presence of hunger. All kinds of external factors may also be involved: whether the sun is shining, childhood likes or dislikes, the company at the table or the comfort of the surroundings. But the whole psychology of well-being at table is too individual and personal to allow easy generalization, so here I'm concentrating on the food part of that enjoyment. Happily, this doesn't mean that you have to be a food scientist: my concern is not how the senses work but how to get the greatest reaction from them. After all, one doesn't need to know what is under the bonnet of a car to make it accelerate away.

The Senses

Those sense receptors most obviously engaged in the activity of eating are on the tongue and in the nose, but almost as important are the eyes and parts of the mouth other than the tongue. These last are to my mind responsible for an additional sense, which I've called here, for want of a better description, 'mouth feeling'. Fingertips add something if food is eaten by hand. Even the ears have a role. And there are ancillary factors which keep the senses appreciative far beyond their normal attention span. I'm thinking here of variety of textures and flavours; of novelty and its reassuring opposite, familiarity; and the little-used 'surprise' element. I'll deal with these after the senses.

Taste

It is common to use either 'flavour' or 'taste' when describing food but, to be more exact, the word 'flavour', as defined by the British Standards Institute in 1975, really includes the smell of food as well as its taste.

It is generally recognized that there are four basic taste sensations – sweet, sour, salt and bitter – although some say there are five and some, six (more on this later). The receptors on the tongue that respond to these tastes are the taste buds, of which the average adult has several thousand. They are scattered all over the surface, back and edges of the tongue, but

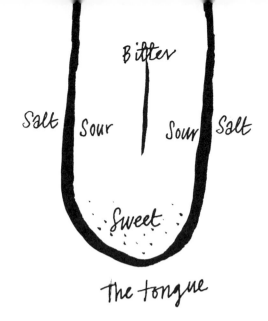

The tongue

there are some areas which seem to be more sensitive to a particular taste than others.

According to American food scientist Harold McGee (*On Food and Cooking*, Allen & Unwin, 1986), for instance, the tip of the tongue is most sensitive to sweetness, either side of the tongue to saltiness, the sides to sourness and across the back to bitterness. My perceptions don't quite agree with this – the areas seem much less defined – but it is a starting point to work out for yourself just where your sensitive areas are. While investigating, you might notice a weaker reaction to one stimulus than the others. That could be a blindness to a specific taste, which is quite a common occurrence.

Taste buds work on a solution of saliva and food particles dissolved by an enzyme in the saliva. When food is present, the eyes, nose and, to some extent, the ears anticipate the needs of the mouth, and the saliva flow increases to speed the process. Since more saliva produces a stronger signal, this 'mouth-watering' sensation is obviously worth encouraging.

Although individual sensory cells in the taste buds regenerate continuously, the number of taste buds declines with age. Babies start off with them all over the mouth – on and under the tongue, on the linings of the cheeks and on the back of the throat. It is hard to imagine what such a formidable array of buds, allied to the exquisitely sensitive nose that babies have, would do for the appetite, but it is no wonder they get impatient when the smell of food is around. The loss of taste buds with age (presumably a natural consequence of the decreasing need for food) could lead to disinterest in eating, at least on a sybaritic level, were it not for a cook's skill at increasing food's potential for stimulation. Since the aged live in a shrinking pool of sense awareness, this is a blessing.

Apart from the generally recognized tastes of sweet, sour, salt and bitter, there are, as already mentioned, two others that are more debatable and much less clearly defined. One is a tongue reaction, variously described as metallic/electric or alkaline. In effect, it's like having a metal such as iron or copper in the mouth. I am usually aware of it when leaving the dentist with a new filling in my mouth. Blood produces a salty version of this 'taste' because of the minerals in it, but the sensation is generally elusive and harder to define than the big four tastes. This taste reaction is not associated with pleasure, so, should you find it

in your food and want to get rid of it, it may help to know that Alan Davidson, speaking at the Oxford Symposium on Taste in 1987, said that the metallic taste (he was talking of copper at the time) seems accentuated in the presence of bitter tannin but is diminished by the other three tastes.

The second taste is much more pleasant. Max Lake has described it in his book *Scents and Sensuality* (John Murray, 1989) as an 'all round the mouth' taste which the Japanese call *umami*. It envelops the tongue in a velvety, slightly salty pleasantness that is almost textural – more of a savoury flatness than a taste. I am aware of it in reduced meat or fish stocks, gelatin, cheese and mushrooms, in tomatoes (especially those delicious sun-dried ones), seaweed, cooked garlic and other members of the onion family. But principally it tastes like MSG, or monosodium glutamate.

Originally extracted from seaweed but now created chemically, MSG has had a bad press, mostly because of its extreme usefulness as a substitute for imagination in creative cooking. A trace of it in food is enhancing, no doubt of that, but if it can be identified, too much has been used. In cheap Chinese 'restaurants', where the food tastes as if salt and MSG are used in equal quantity, it blankets individual tastes, making every dish seem as if it has come from the same pot. Somewhere around one teaspoon per pound (450 g) of meat or six portions of vegetables seems about right. MSG is also notorious because it can give susceptible people a short term pain in the back of the head and cause others to hyperventilate, but such people are a minority.

So much for the tastes in isolation. It is now worth considering a few ground rules that govern the effectiveness of tastes on the taste buds.

Firstly, temperature can enhance or depress the effect of tastes. Bitterness seems at its strongest around 15°C (60°F) and decreases with heat. Sweetness, however, is more pronounced when hot and almost disappears when very cold, which explains why Coca Cola needs to be served near freezing and why, on the first time that I tried to make ice cream, the custard it was made from was so sweet that I thought I'd made a mistake in reading the recipe.

Secondly, some chemicals change their flavour with strength. Too much of the sweetener saccharine tastes bitter, while a very weak salt solution tastes sweet. It is not surprising then to find that sweet and salty complement each other in very unequal amounts, so it is good practice to add a pinch of salt to basically sweet dishes, enhancing sweetness without adding extra calories. And adding a pinch of sugar gives wonderful depth to the flavour of savoury dishes.

Thirdly, the impact of a flavour can be heightened by having more than one of the four tastes in strength. The most obvious enhancement is with sweet and sour. This coupling, found naturally in fruit, is what makes oranges and many other sweet/sharp fruits so delicious. Another vibrant combination is salt and sour, which is one reason why a lemon slice is usually found on a plate of oysters and many other salty dishes. Those who are familiar with Tequila may know this combination at its most sizzling. When the rim of the glass is moistened with lime juice and dipped into salt, it gives the drink a tremendous kick. It must be allowed, to be fair, that the Tequila does have something to do with it. Bitter and sour work together too: for example, if food gets burned, adding a little sourness will help make the bitter taste that results from burning more acceptable. Sweet and salty counteract each other unless present in very unequal amounts.

The way all this can be used to improve the depth of flavour is one of trial and error. Assuming the dish about to be served tastes flat and uninteresting, you'll need to think about the flavour and which of the four tastes would improve its depth. With experience, you will know what to add almost subconsciously, but in the beginning each taste must be tried separately (for lists of ingredients to add that are sharp, sweet, salty or bitter see pp. 80–85). The way to do it without ruining the whole dish is to add a little of the taste that seems lacking to the side of the dish and stir it just enough to flavour a small area. Taste to see what has happened; it will be easy to tell whether that is the one that is needed, but if still in doubt, taste the untreated part and then go back and try the treated part again. If it seems right, then adjust the rest of the dish accordingly; if wrong, then stir that part into the rest, diluting the effect to a background flavour without wrecking the whole dish. It is possible that more than one extra flavour will be needed, so try other areas with the other tastes and match and mix until it seems right. Usually it will be salt, sour or sweet that is missing. Leave testing for bitterness until last; it is the most difficult taste to add by itself and the least likely to be needed.

Bitterness usually finds its way into a dish by way of browning or burning. When you brown ingredients to increase their flavour, a pleasant touch of bitterness comes with it; but if the way you are cooking doesn't include browning and the whole taste seems lacking in body, finding a way to add it is sometimes a bit of a problem. The standard way is to flash the dish under a grill for a quick browning, but not all dishes lend themselves to that treatment. One solution I can offer is to scrape some burnt toast over the dish; it is the nearest I can get to a pure bitter taste. Another enterprising solution, at least for sweet dishes, is to sprinkle sugar over a dish and burn it brown with a blow torch. Fuelled by a small butane gas cylinder, very neat and easily stored, a blow torch leaves no taste behind and can be used to scorch a surface which would be impossible to brown by other means. Even a fruit salad can get a caramel topping this way. To those whose childhood conditioning included some unpleasant experiences with burnt food, all this – actually adding the burnt taste to the food – must seem a bit bizarre, but it is worth remembering that many compulsive foods, coffee or chocolate among them, contain bitterness.

Smell

The sense of smell is much more volatile and personal than that of taste and we know far less about it. There are no clear categories of smell as there are for tastes, only a few generally accepted words – rose, for example – to encapsulate and recall a particular smell; there are no universal preferences for a particular scent, nor can we all smell the same smells.

Selective odour blindness is quite common. In his book *Scents and Sensuality* Max Lake argues that 15 per cent of the population are blind to the 'burnt' smell.

The olfactory nerve-cells are located at the top of the nasal passage, away from the normal flow of air during breathing but more exposed by sniffing, which increases the air flow over them. When eating food, there are two stages to the perception of its smell. The first, most easily recognized, is when an aroma is smelled from food before it arrives in the mouth. Later, when food is swallowed, air exhaled through the nose carries with it a quite different smell from the back of the tongue and from the gastric tract. In this way the aroma of food produces two different sorts of reactions: two smells really.

Smells can evoke the past very vividly, but while an ancient perfume bottle with a lingering trace of perfume may vividly recall a lost love or at least the pain of it, another scent or flavour may recall only the vaguest echo, quite impossible to fix but no less poignant. On my first visit to an Indian restaurant, I was startled by a flavour so potently evocative of another distant and indefinable time that I searched for the ingredient responsible. The scent that I was picking up reminded me of eau-de-Cologne but turned out to be the spice cardamom. I knew, coming from a very English background, that I couldn't have experienced this flavour before and yet.... At the time I believed in reincarnation, so I really thought that here at last was a memory from a previous life. This sense of mystery and wonder came to an abrupt end when I discovered that cardamom is one of the carminative ingredients in gripe water. Who would have thought that relief from wind would leave such an indelible memory.

Recognition of a smell is considerably easier if a name can be found or recalled to label it. But it isn't simple to put a name to something so elusive. Look at the names (right) used by those who have tried to make comprehensive lists of areas of smell and you can see the problems they've had:

Flowery	Floral
Citrus	Ethereal
Resinous	Camphor
Spicy	Musky
Putrid	Putrid
Burnt	Pungent
Peppermint	Pepperminty

(Findley, 1924, quoted in *Pears Cyclopaedia*, 93rd edition, Pelham Books, 1984)

(Amoore, quoted in Harold McGee, *On Food and Cooking*, Allen & Unwin, 1986)

Fruitiness
Cinnamon/clove
Vanilla
Jasmine/geraniums/violets
Stale urine/putrefaction
Mouldiness
Burnt
Camphor
Almonds
Garlic/onions
Fish
Crushed ant
Grassiness/mint

(Max Lake, *Scents and Sensuality*, 1989)

Most of these classifications, on their own, are not readily associated with food, but in small measure they combine with tastes to make good flavours. Even the unlikely ammonia/putrid has a place, for a minute quantity can be pleasant. A decomposed, runny and overripe Camembert cheese can be putridly off-putting, but a ripe one, where the decomposition has just begun, has for most palates, a richer flavour than a firm unripe one.

Sight

You wouldn't immediately think that the colour of food could change the taste of it – that if, for instance, you were given two identical mouthfuls of food, but one coloured red and the other yellow, they would taste different. Yet it seems that we are as suggestible in this as in many other matters. In a taste test given at Reading University by Dr David Thomson, students found that lemon jelly tasted of lemon if it was coloured yellow but positively of raspberry or strawberry if it was coloured pink. And who can doubt that wine drunk from a crystal glass tastes quite different if drunk from a white, opaque plastic cup. In this case it is the loss of transparency that makes the difference; were the plastic cup clear rather than opaque, the difference would be much less pronounced.

Likewise, it would seem that even our favourite food, if coloured oddly, would be unpalatable. During the earlier part of this century a member of the avant-garde Dada movement – a group of artists who were given to exploring sensations – gave a delicious dinner where the major ingredient of each dish was coloured blue. It proved to be quite inedible. Blue is the only sector of the spectrum that seems to have this effect. The reason, I suspect, is that there are no naturally coloured fruits or vegetables that are blue; even with blueberries, it is the bloom rather than the colour of the fruit itself that gives them their name. Very few other foods have a blue colour (one obvious exception, blue cheese, is often only partially blue or, rather, slate green/blue) so when we do come across a food that is even vaguely blue, we instinctively regard it with suspicion.

The appearance of food plays a vital part in arousing anticipation. An attractive-looking dish certainly does this, but too much time spent on decorative artistry can be misguided. It is often more rewarding, both for cook and eater, to have more time spent on creating a flavour than on decoration. There are two reasons for this. The first practical, the second psychological. Firstly, much less time is spent looking at food than eating it, so it is sensible to make an effort where its effect has more time to make an impact. The second reason is all to do with the tempo of a meal. Raising expectations of how food will taste by making it look ravishing is to run the risk of disappointing when it actually gets in the mouth. Much better to understate at the beginning and not 'peak early' as Americans succinctly put it.

Mouth Feeling

There are receptors on the tongue and in the mouth, other than those that react to taste. These register pain, temperature variations and texture, as well as 'chemical heat' – by which I mean the reaction produced by chillies, horseradish, mustard, peppercorns and the like. In small amounts, chemical heat produces a glowing tingle of some pleasure and can have a brightening effect that is very handy in lifting heavy or bland flavours. Sensitivity to chemical heat varies enormously from person to person but tender palates, regularly exposed to it, soon acclimatize.

Capsaicin – the active heat ingredient in chilli – quickly becomes attractive, even compulsive, which may account for the annual consumption of chilli increasing steadily over recent years. Maybe it is attractive because it stimulates digestion or maybe because, when the mouth has been seared with chilli, the brain produces its own pain-killing endorphins, giving a sense of well-being almost as addictive as that produced by jogging. Another argument suggests that the pain warnings given by the receptor cells in the presence of chilli are familiar and controllable (since you can stop eating at will), allowing the tingle of the taste to be enjoyed without fear. The addictive endorphins explanation seems more likely to me.

Whilst on the subject of controllable or familiar dangers, the Japanese delight in eating Fugu, a puffer fish, some parts of which contain toxins so strong that a minute amount makes lips numb and tingling, and more is lethal. Is this the same reaction that chilli gives? Probably not, but if there is one certain way of concentrating the mind on the mouth this must be it. Fugu must taste wonderful.

Receptors in the mouth also register the texture of food. This aspect of eating isn't often thought about consciously, but it is an area begging to be exploited. The teeth are the prime sensors of texture, capable of detecting quite a number of textural effects, ranging from the softest smooth ice-creams, through viscous toffee, low resilience jelly and high resilience rubbery whelks, to crunchy carrots, nuts and crisp crusted bread. It is very effective to have more than one of these textures in a dish. For instance, the smooth creamy texture of a soup commands twice the attention if it has in it some small solids with a textural contrast, such as diced crisp apple or crunchy fried croutons. Indeed, the enjoyment of eating a crisp salad, freshly tossed in its dressing, compared with the doubtful pleasure of eating one where the dressing has been allowed to attack and soften the ingredients underlines the importance of this area. I make as much effort to get vibrant textural contrast as I do to contrasting the flavours between one course and the next.

Other parts of the mouth are important in registering texture too. When the tongue presses food against the roof of the mouth, it produces sensations which have been categorized as dryness, prickliness, sliminess or creaminess. The unpleasant sensation of dryness triggers off chewing, which increases the saliva flow. Extra saliva increases the number of signals reaching the taste buds, so it makes food taste better. You would hardly have thought that prickles in the mouth would be anything other than unpleasant, but the Greeks, either from parsimony or guile, not only pickle capers but separately pickle the soft stalks that carry them. These stalks bear thorns which don't altogether soften down in the pickling process. The first time I came across them was in a Piraeus waterfront café waiting for the next ferry to Crete. Something was giving a quite remarkable lift to what appeared to be a tomato, onion, caper and fresh thyme flower salad, but I didn't immediately associate it with prickles and the pain/pleasure principle until I isolated the thorns. I've used these stalks since to add surprise to an otherwise predictable dish. It gives an effect similar to a pinprick of chemical heat.

Sliminess is really slippery smoothness and thought of in those terms it is quite pleasant. An enjoyable example of sliminess is the well-known wild boletus fungus called cep, which softens down in cooking and gives a slimy texture in the mouth.

Creaminess, as a texture rather than a taste, works all around the mouth, not only between the tongue and the roof of the mouth but between the teeth and cheek linings. When sucking creamy liquids, one is aware that it is harder to clear the mouth than when sucking thin liquids. This is fine, especially if the liquid has a pleasant taste, but the distinction between the two effects is hard to exploit. I do know of an instance where the two appear in the mouth together, and that is when cream is floated on top of coffee. When you drink this combination, the coffee is swallowed fast, but the cream lingers and, if this has been sweetened with a liqueur, then each mouthful delivers two tastes – one after the other. Another instance is with cream floated on consommé or borsch.

Touch

Food that can be easily picked up is more enjoyable eaten with fingers than with cutlery. And no wonder, for the fingertips are the most tactile instruments, deliciously receptive to temperature and texture and therefore capable of alerting other senses to forthcoming pleasures. So, by eating with a knife and fork we deprive the sensory system of a powerful primer and of the enjoyment of sucking – one of the most satisfying, elemental feelings associated with eating and contentment.

I have some Jewish friends, a family with whom I have spent many happy Friday suppers. Naturally, roast chicken is the dish. We start with knives and forks, but afterwards the carcass is put on the table for those who need a little more, when it is attacked with fingers. With everyone being so tactile, an informal atmosphere soon develops, making the chicken taste twice as good – even before the finger-sucking begins.

If our aim is to give maximum impact to our

food, we must dispense with knives and forks. Sticky fingers are not pleasant, I know, but sucking and fingerbowls deal effectively with most of that.

Hearing

In some ways this sense overlaps with mouth feeling. The sound of chewing, transmitted via the jawbone to the ears, becomes amplified and more significant. The compulsive popularity of potato crisps, Chinese prawn crackers, Indian poppadoms and other easy crunchers indicates just how attractive it is to produce loud sounds in the mouth with little effort. And it has to be the sound that does it, judging by the amplification crunchy sounds get in television advertisements for crisps, and the lack of compulsion when these foods lose their crunchiness.

Sounds from without don't have as much appeal as sounds from within unless they are associated with back-up sights and smells. Even the evocative sound of frying doesn't get the saliva flowing unless it is supported by an appropriate smell.

Hearing a sound of one's own making is curiously satisfying, so it is a pity that noisy eating is so frowned on. The Chinese have no such inhibitions: they smack their lips, suck noisily and belch freely after eating, as a sign of appreciation. What a pity we in the West are so inhibited, as it is clear that this, like sucking fingers, is another area where our senses are being deprived.

Ancillary Stimulants

Familiarity

Food which has been consumed regularly in childhood is the food yearned for in 'second childhood'. Childhood food, along with much else, is rejected as we grow and acquire more sophisticated palates, but the memory of things past makes it compulsive later.

Novelty

To produce a sustained impact in the mouth, and sometimes in the memory, food should contain new sensations to awaken senses that have done their guard duty and gone to sleep. Fresh stimulation-triggers need to be built into a meal at short intervals, and the ideal way of doing this is with a meal of small, nicely contrasting dishes each varying in flavour, texture, temperature and colour from the one before. Such a meal keeps attention on the plate where it belongs, if it is to be memorable. Anyone who has experienced a Scandinavian smorgasbord, mezes in a Greek taverna or has been to San Sebastian in Spain for the tapas will know that this formula hits the spot. And how about a chef's tasting menu or a meal of starters alone – not to mention the endless series of small dishes eaten in the East. It seems clear that a meal constructed on the assumption that successive mouthfuls of food are more enjoyable if they are each different in some way is going to be popular worldwide.

Surprise

This is novelty with no visual clues, where the familiar appearance of a dish hides a secret unexpected flavour. An example will serve better than anything else to show what I mean. Nothing looks more predictable than the appearance of a carrot salad. The flavour of raw carrots is familiar, even if you don't know whether the carrots have just been picked and are freshly grated and juicy, or were picked weeks ago, grated yesterday and are as stale and dry as old bread. Imagine, therefore, the jolt to the senses when, expecting to deal only with the quality of the carrot or the balance of the dressing, you taste, out of the blue, a fresh zesty orange taste together with the expected sweetness of the carrots. This version of carrot salad calls for the addition of nearly invisible shreds of orange zest. Little surprises like this, simple in themselves, are dazzlingly effective at bringing the senses back to life.

During the course of a meal I would expect to consciously involve all the senses and ancillary stimulants mentioned here, and this means sitting down with a coffee and planning out tastes, temperatures and textures for contrast between one course and another. I deal with this more fully in Chapter 5 on pages 150–160.

2 Preparing Food

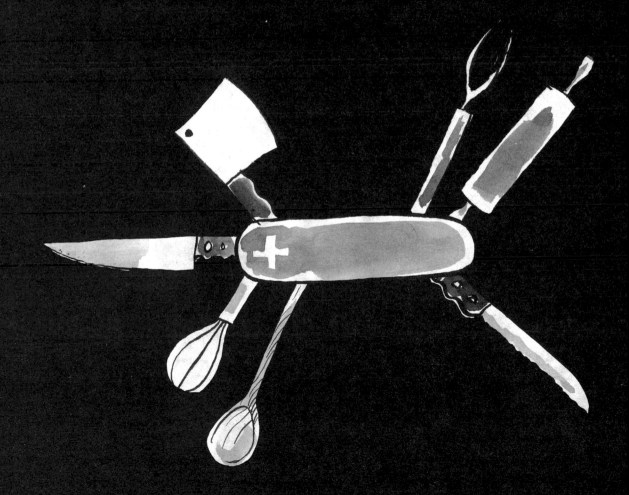

This chapter deals with the processes involved in preparing food: about what can or must be done to make it edible or improve its taste before cooking. Some of these processes change the nature of food enough to make cooking unnecessary. All of them extend the range of flavours or textures available to an imaginative cook.

Salting and Brining

The ancient way of preserving food by covering it in salt (or by covering it in a strong brine solution) works because salt, (or brine) extracts fluid from food by osmosis, both dessicating it and inhibiting any microbe development. The longer in brine the food remains, the more fluid is extracted and the more denatured it becomes. For some reason – part of a folk memory of tastes perhaps – saltiness in food is attractive to us, so even today, when there are other ways of preserving food which do not change its nature so much, the more palatable levels of salting and brining are still used.

Meat

Brining meat gives it an attractive rosy colour in the process. The chemical responsible, nitrite (a component of saltpetre) prevents fat from oxidizing and acts as a powerful anti-bacterial agent as well as adding a piquant flavour. It seems quite probable that these benefits were taken for granted until refined salt – salt with its nitrite removed – became available, when it was discovered that meat lost these benefits and turned an unappetizing grey without it. I mention this because a while ago, nitrite, used at levels necessary for old style preservation, was discovered to be carcinogenic. Happily, recent investigations suggest that, at the reduced levels needed to trigger piquancy and prevent oxidizing and bacterial activity, the risk doesn't outweigh the benefit. Unhappily, nitrite is not easily found, so home brining has to manage without it.

Plain brine (refined salt and water only) tends to be monotonous on the tongue but extra sophistication can be gained by adding sugar or honey and even more by including herbs and spices – peppercorns, bay leaves, juniper and the like.

Since brining normally takes days (or even weeks depending on the type and size of the meat), forward planning – of an order that is usually beyond my organizing – is needed, so I hadn't seriously considered the process until I read Jane Grigson, an inspired cookery writer, on the subject. In her book *Good Things* she uses a quick twelve-hour brining to add character to meat. Brining at speed was a novel idea, but experiment proved it to be all that she had promised. She gave duck as an example, but all poultry benefit from the technique. A battery chicken almost tastes as if it were from a farmyard if given a dip for several hours in a salt/sugar brine before roasting. (See p. 40 for a recipe.) Other white meats (pork, veal or rabbit) are similarly transformed.

Brining is absolutely essential to the smoking process (see below), since it stops fat in the meat from going rancid while subject to the warmth of the smoke.

Fish

Usually fish is salted rather than brined – there is so much liquid present in fish that salt quickly turns to brine anyway – and a quick salting (in much the same way as the quick brining mentioned above for chicken) can be used on fish to delicious effect. The well-known Scandinavian way with herrings (effectively, a two-day dip in sweetened salt) makes them good enough to eat raw, and this same method can be employed on raw salmon to turn it into gravadlax. (See p. 112 for a recipe.)

Vegetables

Salting was one of several ways (drying and bottling being the others) of preserving vegetables before the days of home freezers. Although freezing keeps more of the individual flavour of vegetables, salted vegetables still exist in the folk memory of nostalgic tastes and command a wide following. That well-known European dish, sauerkraut, is basically little more than salted cabbage which has been allowed to ferment. Cabbage is similarly processed in Korea where it is called kimchi. Cabbage also responds to quick brining (although, since it uses vinegar rather than

water in the brine, it could equally be called marinating). A speedy and delicious version of red cabbage pickle can be made in an hour using a brine made of salt, sugar and vinegar, but more importantly, when this relish is stir-fried with garlic oil, it converts into a sauerkraut-like, hot red cabbage side dish, which marries perfectly with jugged hare or boiled mutton. Courgettes, green tomatoes or fine sliced onions are all suitable candidates for this treatment. (See pp. 134–5 for a recipe.)

Marinating

A basic marinade uses a 'bath' of acid, salt, oil and flavourings – virtually a vinaigrette – to tenderize, flavour and temporarily preserve food or, in the case of fish, to 'cook' it. The acid tenderizes the flesh – in fish to such an extent that no further processing is needed. As in salting or brining the salt promotes osmosis by drawing the juices from the flesh and in so doing speeds the penetration of the tenderizing acid. See the recipe for cebiche or marinated raw fish, p. 112.

But marinating can so easily mask the flavour of the foods being processed. Let me pass on a cautionary tale. Some years ago, I got involved in the running of a kebab stall at a 'medieval' fair in Norfolk. Determined to make my kebabs good enough to queue for, I evolved a rich marinade using red wine and lemon juice as the acid content, caramelized soy sauce – I knew no better then – instead of salt and a rather heavy hand with the dried herbs and pepper. Into this muscular brew I placed my cubes of meat – venison in one dish, hogget (one year old lamb, full of flavour) in another – giving both lots a good roll around. Some four hours later, I couldn't tell the cooked venison from the lamb. In large part I blame the red wine for this blanket gameyness. The caramelized soy gave everything the same colour but mostly it was the wine that hacked into the flavours and did the damage, so do take care.

Macerating

Macerating is synonymous with marinating except that it is more often associated with the steeping of fruit, generally in alcohol. This is a practice I thoroughly recommend although care is needed with the timing. Most of us, I imagine, have suffered yesterday's or even this morning's fruit salad. It isn't a happy experience; how quickly the alcohol and sugar syrup attacks the cut fruit, softening and ripening as it goes and producing a textural disaster with one monotonous flavour.

When macerating fruit, timing is all-important; the softer the fruit used, the shorter the steeping time, so if the fruit for a mixed salad is of variable firmness it will need staggered steeping times, sometimes as brief as a minute or two. I've never tasted a better salad than freshly picked raspberries, warmed by the sun, lightly rolled in fine sugar, moistened with

good claret (which accentuates the flavour of the berries) and served within minutes – before the alcohol softens more than the surface of the fruit. The fresh, ripe, but sharp raspberry taste as the fruit is crushed in the mouth combines with the distinctive taste of the macerating claret and sugar to make one luxurious whole. It must be the cedary tannin and light acidity of the red wine that does it. Before my French uncle took me under his tutelage and introduced me to this exquisite liaison, I had thought that lemon juice or even white wine was the best enhancer.

This is macerating in its simplest form with exactly the right ingredients in the syrup for raspberries. Matching the alcohol to the fruit is the all-important finesse. Claret is good with strawberries and other soft red fruit, too, but try sweetened Poire William (a delicious pear-flavoured eau-de-vie) with ripe pears. Other good combinations are the cherry-stone-flavoured liqueur Maraschino with cherries, and Amaretto (made from the kernels of apricots) with ripe apricots. Fruit sugar, which has an uncanny knack of adding ripe fruit sweetness to unripe fruit, is a comparatively recent find for me and is available fairly widely these days.

At the other end of the macerating scale there are fruit salads where macerating is allowed to affect the fruit over quite a considerable period and the fruit surrenders all its flavour to the alcohol. Rumtopf, for instance, calls for a variety of fruits, as they come into season, to be embalmed in sweet rum. This long maceration does give the rum enormous fruity depth but the flavours of the individual fruits are lost. This alcoholic compôte is served with thick cream the following Christmas and is absolutely delicious.

There is a variation of Rumtopf that is worthy of mention. This is an Italian fruit pickle called *mostarda di Cremona* in which firm whole fruit – cherries, pears, plums, small oranges and the like – are macerated in syrup, just like Rumtopf but without the alcohol, and the syrup is flavoured with mustard oil. It is served as a sharp pickle with cold ham, ox tongue, roast pork and poultry. Although I don't make it myself, the ready-made version is very handy. I don't restrict its use to cold or boiled meats but put snippets of it in a fresh fruit salad; use it as a surprise element in warm buttery spinach and pop it in stir-fries – with chicken and green broccoli, for instance.

Smoking

The primitive method of smoking food was to dangle it over a fire made smoky with damp or green wood. Later when chimneys were used to funnel smoke out of the living room or kitchen, they became the ideal place for more contained and concentrated smoking. Even then, there was a tendency for the food to dry out before being properly smoked. That things have become rather more sophisticated nowadays can be seen from this homely description in the *Country Cookbook*, a 1930s American cook book, for constructing a 'smokehouse'.

Dig a circular pit about 3 feet in diameter and 2 feet deep and set a discarded enamel dishpan about 2 feet in diameter in the pit to hold the fire. Use an old sheet of metal, or wood lined with metal, for a pit cover. Dig a trench from the top of the dishpan sloping upwards to the ground level, about 6 feet long and 6 inches wide. Lay stove or drain pipe into the trench fitting the joints well together. Knock out the two heads of a big barrel and set it over the upper end of the pipe. Cover the top of the barrel with canvas or tarpaulin, and then lay boards over the canvas. Cover the pipe well with earth and pile remaining earth around the bottom of the barrel. And then you will have an effective miniature smokehouse in which meat will be safe from being scorched or falling into the fire if a flame should spring up. The dimensions can be varied to suit whatever junk you have to hand. It will hold a pair of hams or a number of smaller pieces, suspended from hooks screwed through the canvas into the boards, or just strung on small sticks laid across the top of the barrel.

After some instruction on brining hams for a month or so and then smoking them for three or four days 'or longer if the smoke isn't heavy', it describes how the smoker should be started: '... making a fire of dry chips in the dishpan, cover with green wood cut small and when the fire is going well tamp it down with damp sawdust or chopped straw, clamp down the cover when you are sure all will keep alight, and let it smoke.'

The flavour will vary according to the fuel

used. Fruit wood has a high reputation and any small pieces, twigs or shavings may be used. Beech, oak or maple are fine. Other smoking mediums used to add their own particular resonance and flavour to the smoke are peat, seaweed, juniper, bay, heather and even pine if done with a light hand – a touch of resin can be pleasant. As with a barbecue, herbs such as thyme, rosemary and fennel can be employed to achieve your own flavour preference. I must emphasize the need for brining before smoking, not only for the extra flavour but also to help prevent warmed fat from going rancid.

All that the above requires is an area of ground and uncomplaining neighbours. For those without such an amenity it is possible to hot-smoke in your kitchen, using an old pan. This is relatively quick but the food does cook as it smokes. Still, it will allow for some 'hands on' experience (see below).

The commercial 'smoking' of fish is at its worst when fish is painted yellow to give the impression of long smoking. Some producers add an artificial smoke-flavoured liquid to this colouring and do not smoke the fish at all. If it weren't so lousy, it would be a joke. It can give no idea of what a professional smoker can achieve. The best I know is Steve Hatt, who plies his trade in Essex Street, Islington, in north London, and his smoked mackerel is a revelation. The pale brown skin peels back to reveal a layer of jelly, lightly covering moist, yet firm, flesh, and – the master touch of a craftsman – the tail is as moist as the head.

Many years ago, I asked him how he managed this. He smiled, went into his smokehouse and returned carrying a rack with fan-shaped indentations in the wood. 'You see,' he said, 'most smokers skewer their fish through the head which leaves the tail, the narrowest part, nearest the heat. Naturally this has to overcook and dry if the thickest part is to be done properly. This rack', he said, pointing to the indentations in the wood, 'holds the mackerel by the tail.' Of course – and the inedible head is nearest the heat. How nicely thought through, and the end-product of this thinking is superb: moist flesh with a delicious jelly, set from the juices, under the skin – 'worth a detour' as one food guide says.

Method for hot smoking in the kitchen

Use an old pan that has seen better days and reserve this for smoking – it won't be much use for anything else afterwards. The only requirement is that the lid should be a tight fit and that it should be at least 4 in (10 cm) deep. Construct in this a perforated support shelf, about 3 in (7.5 cm) from the bottom, which allows free access for the smoke to cure the food to be placed on it; I use a circular piece of perforated metal for the platform and an old corned beef can, with both the top and bottom removed, for the support.

The food to be smoked should be sprinkled with salt and brushed with oil before being put in the pan. Thin fillets of fish, or chicken breast, are ideal for this treatment. If you fancy food

with an oriental twist, sprinkle it with a little four-spice powder.

Put a heaped teaspoon of sugar in the pan, place the food to be smoked on the shelf and ram down the lid – a couple of sheets of newspaper (cut to shape 1 in (2.5 cm) larger than the diameter of the pan) laid between lid and pan is fine to make it tolerably airtight. Keep an eye on this paper while the flame is high – it is a bit of a fire risk.

Heat the pan until the sugar has carbonized and smoke begins to eddy from the pan then turn down the heat and allow the smoke to cure and cook the food. The time this will take depends on the thickness of the food but for a fish fillet about $\frac{1}{2}$ in (1.25 cm) thick 15 minutes will not only cook it through but give a fairly heavy smoke taste.

Using sugar alone gives rather a characterless cure but adding a teaspoon of fennel seed, dried herbs, oak sawdust or even tea straight from the packet makes the final taste more interesting.

Keep the smell out of the house by cooking over a camping stove in the garden.

Maturing

Meat

The fresher the meat, the tougher it is, but if it is allowed to age in anything other than controlled conditions it soon becomes not only soft but rotten. Keeping most meat in cool (1–3°C/34–7°F) dry storage for a period

improves the flavour and makes it more tender. In the best butchers, lamb is kept for a week, beef for up to three. The exception is pork, which is best eaten fresh, since it has more fat than other meat and the deterioration of meat starts with the fat. Also, although pork is kept and sold in its skin to protect the carcass from external bacteria, this protection is broken in the necessary disembowelling process, allowing rapid deterioration to set in.

Game and venison

Game and venison, having very little fat, can be hung for anything from a week in cool conditions to a fortnight in cold. Game birds should be hung with their innards left in. Not only do they develop a richer flavour that way but gutted birds run the risk of contamination. When birds are well hung, the individual flavour of each species is more pronounced.

Fish

Fish doesn't age very well. Keeping it cool does little to stop deterioration or the loss of the firm texture that makes bright-eyed fresh fish so enjoyable. One exception to this rule is Dover sole, where a minimum of two days is thought necessary for its full flavour to develop, at least by the fishermen in Folkestone harbour – and, subsequently, by me. Dover sole is a very firm fish, and when it is really fresh, it is impossible to skin without pulling away small lumps of flesh as well, so it can stand a bit of relaxing deterioration whilst its flavour improves. I've not heard this of any other firm fish – although I'm told that skate improves for a day's keeping, too.

Cheese

Cheese can be roughly divided into categories according to the amount of liquid in the curd, and the maturing and development of flavour varies with each type.

brie

gorgonzola

sage derby

jarlsberg

edam

leyden

Soft unripened (50–80% liquid)

These cheeses are intended to be eaten fresh. They are white soft curds without a pronounced cheese flavour. Typical names are curd, Cottage, Ricotta, Mozzarella, Petit-Suisse or Feta, which is salty from the brine it is kept in.

Soft ripened (50–60% liquid)

These are similar to the above but have added salt. They are formed into flat shapes with a large surface area and exposed to penicillium bacteria of one sort or another (each sort establishes a different final flavour). Over time a soft, white crust develops and the bacteria begin to affect the rest of the cheese, turning it from a white crumbly curd into a creamy semi-liquid with a definite cheese flavour. Correctly treated (maintained at a humid 10°C/50°F), the decomposition of the curd progresses steadily from the crust inwards. Once the cheese approaches maturation, its progress can be slowed by cooling to get maximum 'shelf life'. Bad storage can lead to uneven ripening, dehydration and inferior flavour. Maturing time is 1–3 months. Typical names are Camembert, Brie, Pont l'Evêque and Cambozola.

When buying soft ripe cheeses, you need a compliant retailer who cares for cheese. A good one, knowing they will not be in perfect condition for long, will ask you when the cheese is to be eaten. The alternative, since these retailers are few and far between, is to find a well-run supermarket with decent storage and a caring buyer. Getting a cheese that is nicely ripe (a very personal matter) requires some gentle squeezing and sniffing. Usually these cheeses come in a variety of conditions. There are those that are firm all over with a very white, evenly flat skin – they have a bland taste. Next are those that are firm in the middle, soft near the skin and the edges, with the skin showing signs of colour (cream and beige); they have a light ammonia or fresh hay smell and a rich creamy taste. Finally, there are those that are soft all over, with no detectable firmness, and the skin has brownish patches and threatens to break when pressed firmly (a dipping of the surface near the edges is a sign of dehydration and poor handling); they have a pungent taste and an ammonia smell. This stage is very edible in my book but not if there is shrinkage.

Semi-hard (40–50% liquid)

These are ripened evenly through the cheese by the bacteria present in the curd. Maturing time is anywhere between 3 and 15 months. They are only sold ripe and in cold conditions they have a few weeks' shelf life. Typical names are Gouda, Edam, Port Salut, Gruyère, Stilton and Gorgonzola.

Munster, Ambassador and Livarot fall halfway between soft and semi-hard. They develop a very strong taste in later life which is delicious to some but nose-pegging to the sensitive.

Hard (30–40% liquid)

These are ripened like the semi-hard cheeses (above) and have a maturing time of 6 to 24 months. Typical names are Cheddar, Leicester, mature Gouda and Cheshire. By the time a cheese is a year old it has developed a delicious, lactic acidity and is quite dry and crumbly. If it is too dry, it can be made into stewed cheese (see p. 105).

Very hard (25–30% liquid)

Ripened like semi-hard cheeses (above), these have a maturing time of 12 to 36 months. Typical names are Parmesan, Pecorino/Sardo, Manchego, very mature Gouda. Unless quite young, these are grating cheeses. The flavours are really strong and salty but not pungent. They all possess the taste – the Japanese call it *umami* – that is so useful in bolstering rather plain-tasting food. Buy as much of it as you can: it keeps for ever, and really old cheese is treasure.

Chopping

I consider this technique the single most useful one in the whole pre-cooking canon. This sweeping statement will need some step by step back-up. Cutting tough long fibres of meat or vegetables into short lengths makes them more manageable in the mouth. The teeth find it a simple matter to separate one short fibre from another, but grinding long fibres into smaller, more swallowable lengths involves a lot of chewing, and that equates with 'toughness'. So, shortening the fibres tenderizes the food, and the simplest and best way of shortening it is with a sharp knife. Simplest, because a knife is easy to keep sharp and clean, and best, because mechanical processors which shorten fibre don't do it as cleanly. Usually they tear, mangle or purée instead, and this means loss of vitamins in vegetables and loss of juice in meat.

The knife

The steel from which a knife is made comes in two basic forms – carbon steel and stainless steel. Ordinary carbon steel is more easily sharpened but it rusts. This can be controlled by wiping the blade with acid, which to a certain extent anneals the surface and stops rust forming so quickly. I find a squeezed-out lemon works well, it discolours the steel but, if you can stand the look of it, it saves on care.

Stainless steel comes in varying qualities. Some, usually the cheapest, are so hopeless that they won't take an edge at all or not for long. Others do better, seeming to need almost no sharpening. As a rule, the thinner the blade, the poorer the quality. Of course stainless steel remains stainless regardless of quality. Manufacturers are more accountable for their claims these days, so it is safe to assume that, if they claim a knife will stay sharp for a lifetime, it will stay sharp for a month or two. These knives often have a serrated edge which starts by

cutting sharply but soon begins to tear food rather than cut it. Although this is still adequate for slicing bread and other short-fibred foods, it makes a messy job of foods with longer fibres, abrading surfaces and causing loss of fluids. Slicing meat thinly is impossible with a blunt, serrated knife.

The shape and size of any blade should be governed by the job the knife is to do. When it comes to chopping and slicing, no matter how small the amount to be dealt with, a full-size chopping knife, designed for the purpose, is the quickest and safest since its fat handle gives more control and less fatigue. Keep small knives with small handles for small, picky jobs where a point as well as a cutting edge is needed.

The traditional French triangular blade is hard to beat. It is at least 6 in (15 cm) long – I prefer 8–10 in (20–25 cm) with a larger handle that is an inch (2.5 cm) from the chopping board when the cutting edge is resting on it. This inch is where your knife-holding knuckles will be, well away from the board. The depth of blade at the handle end (usually 2 in/5 cm) allows the knuckles of the hand holding the food to rest against it as it moves up and down. As long as the knuckles stay in contact with the blade, it is impossible for the fingertips pushing the food towards it to move any further forward than vertical – they can't get under the blade, and the thumb is controlling the food from behind, safe from harm. Once this hand position has been mastered, this technique enables a pretty impressive speed of chopping.

serrated bread knife

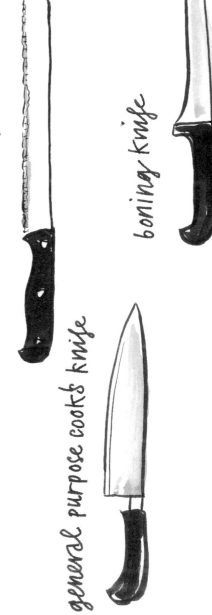

general purpose cooks knife

boning knife

round-tipped ham slicing knife

heavy-duty meat cleaver

chinese slicing knife

chinese carbon steel cleaver

Where the blade movement is only an inch from the chopping board – as for chopping herbs, garlic and small cucumbers – it is possible to get in about five chops a second with complete safety. The sharper the blade, the easier it is of course.

If you can bring yourself to try a Chinese cleaver, it is very easily controlled. It has a fat cylindrical handle, enabling a wonderfully firm and tireless grip, but the asset that makes this my favourite chopping knife is the depth of blade. Not only does it allow the guide knuckles constant contact with the blade but its large surface area allows you to scoop up a large amount of chopped material from the chopping board and transfer it into the pan without spillage. It is no longer necessary to lift the chopping board and scrape the chopped food off it – a slower, more tiring and often messier business altogether. These cleavers, obtainable at Chinese supermarkets, come in several thicknesses of blade, from a heavy bone cruncher to a light vegetable slicer. They take an edge like a razor, but when you have a safe chopping technique this need not frighten but delight.

Meat

When a blade cuts across meat fibres, it makes the meat more tender. A blunt edge presses down on meat whilst cutting it, and juices are squeezed out; a sharp edge needs less pressure to cut, and less juice is lost. If meat is to be reduced small enough to resemble mince, it can be argued that it is easier to put it through a machine processor than chop it with a knife. But a processor tears at the flesh – its knife has a serrated edge – releasing juice and, what is more, it tears unevenly so that at least part of the meat gets pulverized, while larger lumps are reduced. And it is all too easy to over-process the meat, reducing any texture to a featureless purée.

Vegetables

If a food processor is bad for meat, it is worse for vegetables. The processor blade whizzes round, relying on speed to reduce the vegetables. This battering leaves broken and bruised, rather than cut, edges, which start deteriorating much faster because of their increased surface area. This may not matter too much if the vegetable is to be used straight away.

When it comes to onions, however, processors can cause even more problems. The onion family contain in their cells two chemicals which are normally kept separate by the cell walls. When the walls are breached by cutting, these chemicals combine to produce a most unpleasant compound, which deteriorates rapidly when exposed to air. This compound produces the noxious smells, bad breath, indigestion and the general bad press associated with garlic and onions. A garlic press is potentially a worse offender than a food processor since it crushes the cell walls. Usually, when the pressed garlic is cooked straight away, there is no time for deterioration to develop but it is hard not to notice the smell of a stale, used garlic press. The clean cut of a sharp knife reduces this hazard considerably.

One of the things that amused us a lot in the restaurant was a client saying that the reason they returned regularly was because we didn't use garlic. Of course, we used garlic by the sackful, but we used sharp knives to deal with it and only at the last minute.

Radiation

It's early days for this process which, like the microwave, may well come into its own in due course. Uncooked food is irradiated to improve its longevity on the shelf with variable effect on flavour.

At one reported tasting of irradiated food, meat (beef in particular), fish (but not prawns), chicken and cheese all benefited both in taste and texture – astoundingly so in the case of Camembert. Vegetables were not so fortunate apart from lettuce. Radiation also ripens some fruit, especially soft fruit like strawberries, but it isn't so effective with peaches.

3 Cooking Techniques

The most effective way of changing the nature of raw food, to make it edible and more attractive to eat, is to apply heat – in other words to cook it. There are five traditional ways of cooking food – grilling, roasting or baking, boiling, steaming and frying – and what distinguishes one method from another is the medium by which heat is transmitted to the food to cook it. In grilling and roasting heat is transferred by infra-red rays and hot air, in boiling and steaming by water or steam and in frying by oil or fat.

Recent developments, which have accelerated cooking times, such as fan-assisted ovens, pressure cookers and the like, can be seen as improvements to existing methods, but the latest, the microwave, is sufficiently different to be considered worthy of a category of its own. All other ways of cooking start heating food from its surface inwards, but in microwaving radio waves penetrate up to two inches into food, causing fat and water molecules to vibrate and bump into one another and producing enough frictional heat to cook the food from the inside. This makes microwaving truly innovative. It can't brown food, at least not while there is moisture in it, and this is a deficiency as we shall see, but what it can do, superbly well, is to make food steam in its own juice at speed.

Regardless of the technique responsible, one of the best ways of increasing the taste of food is to brown it. Take white sugar; browning or caramelizing it turns it into brown toffee and, while doing so, increases its flavour. Exactly why this is so is still not fully understood. In 1912 a Frenchman, Louis-Camille Maillard, discovered the chemical reaction that takes place when a mixture of amino acid and sugar is heated. When this mixture is browned, its molecules break down and recombine into many other reactive products, which produce intense, and mostly enjoyable, flavours in the mouth. In all probability it is the sheer number of these by-products that accounts for the vivid reaction they get from the palate.

Whatever the scientific reason, there is no doubt at all of the effectiveness of this Maillard reaction, as it is now called. Browning is responsible for the delicious extra taste in a crust of bread; for the very acceptable taste that roasting chocolate and coffee beans produces; for the extra tastiness of browned nuts and other seed kernels; and for the compulsive edge that chips or French fries have over a plain boiled potato.

There are two important points to remember about browning. Firstly, both caramelizing and the Maillard effect only happen at relatively high temperatures (150°C/300°F and upwards), so while there is any moisture left on, or near, the surface of food, any heat around will be turning that moisture into steam and the temperature of the food will be kept down to around 100°C (212°F). It follows then that the surface has to be dry before browning can start. Secondly, these powerful brown tastes flatten – drown might be a better word – other, more individual flavours in food and should, therefore, be used with discrimination.

The characteristics of each cooking technique – the accumulated knowledge on each way of cooking – are most easily illustrated by example. I have used recipes in some cases to do this, and I've quite deliberately chosen widely known ones, for two good reasons. My approach concentrates on the 'sense appeal' of a dish – which senses it appeals to and why – so, even if the recipe is familiar, this should prompt a new way of looking at it. And, secondly, if the reader already knows the basic taste of the dish, it will be much less taxing to imagine what each stage of preparation adds to its final taste and texture (rather like a jigsaw puzzle, which is so much easier if the whole picture is known). Imagining tastes and textures while reading the recipe is splendid training for thinking through tastes when composing completely new dishes.

In the recipes instructions have been separated from the comment to allow practised cooks to establish quickly what sort of dish it is without the tedium of reading basic do's and don'ts, which others will find essential. And for cooks who know how to follow a recipe but are rather too familiar with the end result there are ideas on how to move things around.

Grilling

With grilling (or broiling) the main method of heat transfer from the heat source is by infrared radiation, but when the heat source is under the food to be cooked (as in grilling over an open fire or barbecue), hot air rising as convected heat plays a part as well. Since air is a poor conductor of heat, its effect can largely be discounted in the short-term grilling of thinnish foods but it plays a more significant role in the roasting of a large joint, or carcass, over a dying fire.

Grilling over a wood fire, or barbecueing, is of course the technique *par excellence* for cooking small pieces of poultry, fish and the more tender, short-grained cuts of meat. There is something very compelling and anticipatory about the smell of wood and charcoal smoke – especially combined with the acrid smell of fat burning. Since grilling has been with us for so long, it is quite probable that a reaction to this smell is now built into our subconscious reflexes in some way. I've seen thirsty men pulled away from a bar by the smell of barbecue smoke even before actual cooking began.

Apart from the smoke, when food is barbecued it gets another flavour boost from being seared by the hot metal rack which supports it over the fire. A conventional grill can't give this flavour (if it did, the whole surface of the food would be blackened), so some professional cooks, without a barbecue but knowing what a terrific taste-enhancer it is, sear their food with a red hot grid-iron or a salamander instead. These handy tools – the first a flat metal plate with raised parallel ridges, the second an enlarged version of a flat fork with many tines – are normally used on meat or fish but are also very effective in burning patterns on Feta cheese and for making the best toast in the world.

Kebabs

Serves 4
$1\frac{1}{2}$ lb (680 g) of fairly lean lamb
2 lemons or some green chilli pickle
$\frac{1}{2}$ oz (15 g) sea salt
4 oz (115 ml) vinaigrette (made with lemon juice
*   not vinegar: see p. 132)*
1 tablespoon smoky flavoured dried herb (like
*   thyme)*
1 tablespoon garlic oil (see p. 165) or 1 large clove
*   garlic crushed in oil*
4 large pittas or 2 oz (55 g) of rice (boiled and
*   well flavoured)*
1 large tomato (optional)
1 small handful of chopped parsley

Cut the lamb into roughly 1 in×1 in×$\frac{1}{2}$ in
(3×3×1.5 cm) pieces with the $\frac{1}{2}$ in (1.5 cm) cut
across the grain. Dress with the vinaigrette and
leave for at least an hour.

Push the pieces of lamb onto metal or
wooden skewers, but don't press them tightly
together. Paint the meat with garlic oil and
sprinkle it with salt, then lightly roll the
skewers in a smoky-flavoured dried herb such
as thyme, sage or rosemary – or all three, come
to that.

Barbecue fairly fiercely to get the herb well
scorched, then not so fiercely until all the
exposed edges of the meat are nicely brown, at
which point the meat should be cooked. Move
the meat along the skewer both to loosen its
grip and to check that it is cooked enough
around the skewer.

Accompany the meat with a freshly made relish, such as one made from finely chopped spring onion and a green herb like parsley, or with a green chilli pickle (see pp. 134–5), although just a sprinkle of salt and a segment of lemon would be fine. Serve with flat pitta bread, toasted lightly brown and a little smoky on the barbecue, or with well-flavoured rice, mixed with chopped parsley and fresh, raw, fine-chopped tomato.

How the recipe works

The suggested size of the meat cubes allows for an average barbecue heat; one cut ($\frac{1}{2}$ in/1.5 cm) across the grain) shortens the tough fibres making the meat more tender. Obviously smaller pieces of meat cook through faster, so to get the surface of the meat brown and not overcook the inside would need a pretty fierce fire. Conversely, larger pieces take longer and need a slower fire to allow the meat to cook through without blackening the surfaces.

An hour in the vinaigrette allows the surface of the lamb to be marinated but not the interior – marinate it for too long and the pure lamb flavour is lost. The marinating can be speeded up by cutting the meat smaller, if you're in a hurry.

Garlic oil (raw cloves of garlic blended in oil) is a safe way of adding garlic's delicious depth to food without the side effects that make it taboo to sensitive eaters.

The dried herb, when burnt, adds a touch of bitterness and the smoke from it adds aroma too. Browning the meat gives the Maillard effect described above. Finally, relishes add colour, succulence and brightness in the mouth, which is especially important if only bread is served with the meat. The tomato in the rice does much the same.

Sense appeal

The following thoughts on sense stimulation will indicate how to start thinking about enlivening a dish if it seems a little flat, a little familiar and lacking in surprise, or promising more than it delivers.

Taste All four kinds of taste are catered for. There is not much sweetness but having all four tastes in equal strength leads to anonymity of flavour anyway. *Umami*, the all-round-the-mouth flavour of the fifth taste (see p. 10) is provided by the meat juices.

Smell Even if the sledgehammer smell of the aromatic wood/fat smoke is disregarded, there are many other aromas ranging from the ethereal lemon to the warm bread smell.

Appearance There is plenty of visual excitement: from the pink and brown of the meat to the green, white and yellow of the herbs, onions and lemon.

Touch The warmth and firm, baked feel of the pitta bread is deeply satisfying to the touch, as can be sucking the fingertips clean. Even if you decide on rice, there is no need to use a fork. Eating cooked loose rice with fingers is not the easiest thing to do, but if the rice isn't rinsed after cooking it will lump up quite nicely and a little overcooking makes it hang together even better.

Sound The preparatory sizzling sounds of the grill are followed by the small, succulent sounds of teeth squeezing out juice from the meat and the crunch of the onions.

Adjustments This dish is a powerful stimulus to the senses already but if you feel that it needs further clout it could be enhanced by adding more colour. Here is where accompaniments lend a hand. When I was involved in selling kebabs professionally, we separated all the colours into different dishes: one for onions, one for parsley, one for lemons and one for a red relish – made from tomatoes, peppers and a little red chilli.

The sound could be augmented with crunch from chopped celery or water chestnut, or, even better, from chopped dessert apple, which would also bolster the sweet taste occasionally as it is bitten into.

Changing the ingredients

If every ingredient in this recipe were changed, the dish would be just as appealing, provided the changes gave the same stimulus to the senses.

Meat In Greece and much of the Middle East lamb is the traditional meat. Where beef is available, the more tender cuts work admirably. Coarser cuts can be tenderized by mincing or, better still, by fine chopping (this way the structure is less mangled and more juices are retained). Mince is easily moulded around a skewer; when heated, its juices are lost quickly but juiciness can be added elsewhere – with the relishes for instance. Veal, pork or poultry make very satisfactory substitutes too.

Fish Fish can be grilled on the bone and served with rice but if it is to be tucked into a pitta, it will need filleting first. With fillets as thin as they usually are, a very fast fire will be needed if the outside is to be brown before the inside is overcooked – if they are really thin, consider browning one side only and lightly searing the other. Fish will be pickled by the marinade if it is left there for too long (think of it as a dip in the marinade rather than a soak).

Vegetables It is quite common to mix meat and vegetables together on the same skewer before grilling but, pretty as they look, the idea is ill founded. The cut surfaces of juicy vegetables (peppers, tomatoes, onions etc.) take so long to dry and brown that, when they do, the meat will be overcooked. Better to make separate skewers of mixed vegetables, and grill them fast – to scorch and almost blacken the edges – then move them to a slower heat to soften, occasionally dressing them with vinaigrette. The scorched edges are particularly delicious, especially those of peppers and sweet Spanish onions.

Seasonings Something else salty could replace the sea salt that I've suggested in the recipe: olive purée, mashed anchovies or soy sauce perhaps. There are alternatives to all the ingredients in a vinaigrette. Lists of possible substitutions for salt will be found on pp. 81–2. Add these in penny pinches, as you should in all experiments, or court disaster. Almost nothing will be so bad that a very small amount of it can't be mixed into the whole, sometimes with amazing effects.

Herbs The first kebab I tasted, when the world was young, had whole dried coriander seed pressed in between each chunk of meat. I'd eaten grilled meat before, so although its taste was good, it wasn't novel, but the coriander came as a complete surprise and was a bomb-shell of flavour. It led to an earnest con-versation with the chef – they usually enjoy this sort of interest (I'm flattered when it happens to me) – and I left the café exhilarated by the discovery and, in my pocket, a sample to experiment with. See coriander on p. 87.

Postscript

Barbecues are perverse creatures – slow to start and tending to die just when they are needed most. After a few sessions of blowing until I was dizzy and then flapping frantically with a newspaper, I found the best manipulator to prod sleepy charcoal into life is an electric hair dryer.

Roasting

The words, 'roasting' and 'baking', are to a certain extent synonymous. They both nor-mally refer to cooking in an oven, but roasting is usually connected with the cooking of meat, poultry and peeled vegetables, while baking is associated with breads, cakes, puddings and pastries and with unpeeled potatoes, onions and the like. So for ease of reference I have given a separate section for baking, which follows this one.

The chief difference between roasting and grilling is that in an oven heat cooks food all round rather than one side at a time. This makes roasting faster for large pieces of meat that would take hours, and much turning, on a grill. Soufflés would be non-starters without the oven's all-round heat too.

Roast chicken

Recipes for roasting chicken are commonplace but this one, as with other recipes in this book, is flexible, offering different ways of making this old favourite sparkle without needing to learn a completely new recipe.

Serves 4
3½ lb (1.6 kg) oven-ready chicken (add ½ lb/225 g
*   for every extra person)*
7½ oz (215 g) sea salt (to make 2½ pints/1.4 litres
*   of brine)*
a good handful of fresh tarragon or 2 teaspoons
*   of dried tarragon*
2 tablespoons garlic oil
3–4 fl oz (about 100 ml) each of chicken stock and
*   white wine*

Dissolve the salt in water to make a light brine and submerge the chicken in it for one or two hours. Then drain and dry the chicken (see Brining pp. 20–21).

Loosen the skin over the breasts and thighs and under it spread a handful of fresh tarragon. Paint the skin with fresh garlic oil and dredge with flour.

Finding your way in between the flesh and the skin of a chicken to insert flavourings can be difficult; I find it easier to start at the neck end. Use a finger to ease between skin and flesh and work it, under the skin, around to the outside of the thigh, then up and forward onto the breast. Once the skin is loosened it is easy to introduce the flavourings. Powders can be dropped down in between the skin and flesh, and herbs can be pushed in with the fingertip, working them over the breast and around to the outside of the thigh.

Put the bird on its side in a shallow-sided tray – that is with one breast resting in the tray. Prick the skin with a course needle on those parts most exposed to the heat and put the bird into a hot oven (220°C/425°F/Gas Mark 7). Cook until sizzling can be heard (about 20 minutes), turn the bird onto its other breast, baste with oil from the tray or with extra garlic oil, prick any skin blisters, reduce the temperature to moderate (180°C/350°F/Gas Mark 4) and cook for about 40 minutes. Turn up the heat (220°C/425°F/Gas Mark 7), turn the bird breast side up, so that it is resting on its back, lightly dredge with flour, prick and baste again. In about 10–15 minutes the bird should be nicely browned, and if repeatedly basted it will have a sheen as well. Allow about 1–1¼ hrs in all. For birds over 3½ lbs (1.6 kg), add 15 minutes per lb (455 g) to the cooking time. After cooking it does the chicken no harm at all to rest in a warm place for 20 minutes.

If a roast chicken is to be carved at table there is a way of checking beforehand to see if the bird is cooked through without ruining its appearance. Push a needle or skewer into the thickest part of the breast and watch the juices that flow out. If they are pink, it is nowhere near done; if clear, then the breasts, at least, are done. Investigate the outside thigh in the same way.

If the bird is to be carved out of sight, the safest way to check whether it is cooked is to cut the skin between breast and leg and prise the leg down and away from the carcass. If it is going to be undercooked anywhere, it will be on the inside thigh, where the leg joins the carcass. If the meat exposed looks too pink, cut off both legs – there is a joint to cut through just where it is needed – and put them back in the oven, cut side up, for a few minutes more.

Make the sauce from the residual fat and juices in the pan, mixed with half white wine and half rich, glutinous chicken stock. Emulsify any floating fat into the sauce by giving it a good rolling boil. If necessary, add a little corn-flour (up to 1 teaspoon should be enough to deal with what is likely to be somewhere around 7 fl oz/200 ml of sauce) to keep the fat emulsified. Taste for salt, sugar, pepper. Brighten the flavour with chopped fresh herb, chopped spring onions or scallions, or with other sympathetic, fresh-tasting flavours. Serve with your usual accompaniments; I like roasted vegetables in season and a crisp salad.

If you're roasting anyway and the oven is nicely hot, it is simplicity itself to roast a few vegetables at the same time. First parboil them, then slip them into the roasting tray with the joint or bird halfway through the roasting time, so that they pick up the flavour of the fat and juices. They make very good eating indeed. Root vegetables are the natural candidates for roasting but onions are excellent too. See pp. 128–9 for recipes.

How the recipe works

Sea salt is used for the brine because it tastes saltier and is less chemical. (More than two hours in brine at the salinity given in this recipe could be overdoing it; dilute it to half strength if it is more convenient to brine overnight.) Some people quite like the addition of sugar – a quarter of the amount of salt used (i.e. about 2 oz/55 g or a tablespoonful) is more than enough for me. Drying the carcass afterwards makes it easier to handle and allows the oil to adhere to the skin.

Putting extra flavourings under the skin makes their presence in the flesh more obvious; the skin holds them in place and, when carved, there is a good chance that the flavouring will be there, in place, looking very pretty on the plate. Green herbs, in particular, look most attractive against the brown skin and the white flesh.

Painting the skin with some sort of oil or fat prevents burning; bacon laid on the breast does the same thing. The original reason for using bacon in this way was to stop the breast from becoming too hot and drying out – a real danger if the bird is kept breast up for all the roasting time. Garlic oil enhances appearance, as it leaves flecks of browned garlic over the skin and also adds an almost nutty richness. Flour dredged over the skin gives extra browning potential. A shallow tray allows the heat to circulate and brown the bird more completely than a deep-sided one. For a really rapid roast, with all-round browning, sit the roast on a wire shelf above the tray – messy, but the result is good.

The reduction in oven temperature after the initial sizzling is needed because of the fixed rate at which the body fluids can transfer heat from the outside to the interior of the roast. To continue applying heat at a greater rate only dries out the exterior more than is needed without increasing the heat penetration time very much. Extra heat at the end of the roasting browns the breast skin nicely.

> Toughness in meat comes in two forms, only one of which can be dealt with by roasting. The chewy gristle (or collagen) of the connecting tissue needs heating for some time to convert it into soft gelatin, and during that time the muscle overcooks and loses its juicy succulence. However, the flavour of tough meat is much superior to tender, and sauce can replace its missing succulence. The other toughness is of coarse-fibred muscle. This can be remedied by carving the cooked meat across the grain, in slices as thin as the sharpness of the carving knife will allow. Coarse fibre, in lengths no longer than the thickness of a slice, breaks up quickly when chewed and is then easy to swallow – tender in other words.

As for making the sauce, there is usually more fat than body juices left in the tray once roasting has finished. Emulsifying at least some of this into the sauce will thicken it and improve its taste and texture in the mouth. The acidity in the white wine helps emulsify the fat. Rapid boiling breaks up the fat into mol-ecules and a glutinous chicken stock holds it in suspension. Sometimes, if there is too much fat or the stock isn't quite glutinous enough to hold an emulsion, a thickening agent – like cornflour – can be employed to hold the suspension of fat. Too rich a chicken sauce can be cloying, and this can be cut with a few sparkles of fresh uncooked herb, a little fine-grated lemon or orange zest, or the last-minute addition of fine chopped carrot, chives or spring onion. Adjusting the flavour and texture of a sauce, and dealing with excess fat, is discussed more fully on pp. 70–72.

Many people associate roast chicken with a stuffing placed in the cavity of the bird before cooking, to add the extra flavour that I have put under the skin. This means that the bird will have to be roasted long enough for the stuffing to get at least heated through. Since the heat passes through the bird to get to the stuffing the flesh will be overcooked. Better by far to make the stuffing into balls and brown them in the pan alongside the chicken, but it isn't really necessary if you have used herbs under the skin.

Sense appeal

Taste The flavours in the mouth will be nicely rounded because the sauce has already been adjusted for that. Also the *umami* all-round-the-mouth taste, which comes from many sources but mostly the glutinous stock, will enhance the flavour. The browned skin adds the Maillard effect.

Smell Freshly roasted chicken with a herby overtone is almost enough by itself, let alone the fresh fragrance of the 'brighteners' in the sauce.

Appearance This dish has some colour. The creamy flesh of the chicken is a little pink – a side-effect of the brining – the skin should be brown and shiny with little flecks of browned garlic. The green herb will be glinting through the skin. The sauce is a paler brown, almost beige, with a surface sheen from the emulsified fat, but clearly these colours are in close harmony and this dish will have to rely on the accompaniments for contrasting colour. This needs to be thought out at the planning stage. A bright green vegetable or salad – served with the chicken rather than afterwards – would help; a rice made yellow with turmeric or saffron, together with a raw chopped tomato or red capsicum topping, would help a lot more.

Mouth feeling The succulent chew of the flesh, the mealy rice or potatoes and the crunch of the raw brighteners will help focus attention on the whole dish.

Changing the ingredients

Meat Although this recipe is for chicken, and
the details of cooking and preparing the sauce
have all been written with chicken in mind,
much the same technique can be used for roasting any domestic bird or piece of meat.

Quick brining is a positive improvement
with any flesh that could be thought of as
bland, and most white meats – pork, veal, baby
lamb and even domesticated rabbit – come into
this category. Red meats are improved too, but
joints with large surface areas of cut muscle
lose blood in the brining, so with them it is
preferable to rub the cut surfaces with salt
before cooking or, better, add a few grains of
salt to the cut slices of cooked meat immediately before serving. Fat is much improved with
salt, it pulls out its flavour, and with fatty
birds – I'm thinking of duck and goose here –
the extra flavour acquired by brining is remarkable.

Pork is the only meat sold with its skin on
and there are two ways of using this bounty if
you are roasting the meat. Either it can be
removed and used to make a gelatinous stock –
rich with the desirable *umami* all-round-the-
mouth taste – or it can be converted into crackling. See p. 142 for recipe.

Herbs and flavourings Where tarragon was put
under the skin, consider using other fresh
herbs – almost any of them will do here. Dried
herbs are good, but they are stronger tasting
than fresh so use accordingly.

Fresh ground spices are a possibility. With
chicken, think about coriander, mace or
pepper. Fresh shreds of lemon zest with ground
coriander make an intriguing combination and
the zest looks good under the skin. See p. 121
for other alternatives, like olive purée. Paprika
chicken (p. 122) also uses this recipe.
–   With joints of meat, where there is no such
convenient covering under which to tuck flavours, pierce the joint with a narrow blade and
stuff the extra flavours into the wound.

Baking

To illustrate baking I've chosen two types of
soufflé and a sponge pudding that has been with
me since nursery days.

To see at the dinner table a soufflé that is
towering, glossy brown and slightly quivering
should arouse anticipatory juices in the most
jaded of palates. It is impressive but not as
difficult as you might think. For absolute perfection, a soufflé should be sufficiently moist
inside to need no sauce, and this requires
exquisite timing and accuracy of oven temperature.

A soufflé is really nothing more than a quite
thick, well-flavoured sauce or a purée – both
usually enriched with egg yolks – into which
well-beaten egg whites are tenderly folded.
This mixture is poured into a warm, buttered
dish with fairly deep sides and then placed in
a moderately hot oven until it expands and
browns on top and is just set inside. The sauce
is usually a warm béchamel (see p. 130), com-

bined with egg yolks and whatever flavourings you had in mind, while the purée is made from fruit, vegetables, fish or even ham or chicken. When the yolks are incorporated, the mixture, either sauce or purée, should be thin enough to pour. It will be quite satisfactory if this base mixture is made the day before it is needed – as long as it is at room temperature when it is eventually used.

Correctly beaten, egg whites should expand to seven times their original volume. It will help if the whites are at room temperature, reasonably fresh, completely yolk free and beaten in a copper bowl, which adds copper ions to the mix and makes it more stable (a small pinch of cream of tartar per each egg

white will have the same effect). Equally, the utensils should be completely fat free, clean and dry. Salt or sugar, if needed, should be added nearer the end than the beginning of beating since they inhibit foaming.

Overbeating – easily done with an electric beater – makes the whites difficult to combine with the sauce and considerably less stable, by which I mean that the foamy mass is less able to hold the bubble walls and it starts to drain. Perfectly beaten whites should be glossy to look at and hold a soft peak. When the beater is taken from the foam it will pull up a small peak which should just topple over; if it continues to point upwards, you've gone too far and will have to hurry.

A soufflé sufficient for four takes around 30 minutes to bake – an inconvenient time; too long to start baking after the previous course has been cleared but too short to start baking before the previous course is served. This stumbling block may be overcome by cooking individual soufflés in small ramekins which take around 10 minutes in the oven – time enough to get people settled at the table if the soufflé starts the meal and not too long to wait in between courses. Ramekins $3\frac{1}{2}$ in (9 cm) in diameter by $1\frac{1}{2}$ in (4 cm) deep are a good size for a starter or for a savoury after the main course.

So much for the generalities of soufflé and sponge making. Of the three recipes, the first is a cheese soufflé using béchamel sauce; the second, a raspberry soufflé using a fruit purée; and the third, which is a lovely example of the technique, is neither a soufflé nor a sponge – called in my mother's collection of recipes 'delicious lemon pudding'.

Cheese soufflé

Serves 4
1 oz (30 g) butter
1 oz (30 g) flour
$\frac{1}{2}$ pt (285 ml) milk
2 oz (55 g) grated Parmesan cheese
1 oz (30 g) grated mature Cheddar (optional)
4 egg yolks
5 egg whites
seasoning to taste

Make a béchamel sauce with the butter, flour and milk (for more on béchamel see p.130). While it is warm and slack, stir in the grated cheeses and 4 well beaten egg yolks. Add salt to taste, a fair amount of pepper and consider adding a pinch of nutmeg, mace or chilli for an additional lift.

Whip the 5 egg whites to a soft peak and fold tenderly into the warm cheese sauce.

Pour thickly into a warm, buttered $1\frac{1}{2}$ pt (850 ml) soufflé dish, run a knife through the surface of the mixture about 1 in (2.5 cm) in from the edge, to create a weakness there, and place the dish on a baking tray two thirds of the way down the oven, pre-heated to 200°C/400°F/Gas Mark 6, for 23–25 minutes.

Alternatively this quantity will make 6 individual soufflés, in $3\frac{1}{2}\times1\frac{1}{2}$ in (9×4 cm) ramekins, and take about 10 minutes in the oven.

How the recipe works

When beaten well, egg yolks take in air which

adds to the general lightness, but it is a counsel of perfection. Salt should be added after the cheese since that is salty already. A warm sauce is slacker than a cold one, making it easier to fold in the whipped whites. The pepper and mace add aroma; the chilli – whether fresh and very finely chopped or, less effectively, as cayenne powder – adds brightness to cut the richness of the cheese.

The extra egg white is to ensure a decent rise of the crust. Folding in 'tenderly' usually means first adding a quarter of the whites to the sauce and mixing in well. This loosens the sauce to allow the remainder of the whites to be folded in more lightly. A heavy hand is death at this point. Don't overdo the folding in; the mixture doesn't have to be perfectly blended. It should be a thick bubbly mix that pours, slightly reluctantly, into the dish.

The soufflé dish is buttered to lubricate the rise of the soufflé and warmed to get the base of the soufflé off to a good start. Making a cut in the surface provides a weakness in the hardening crust so that it can break if the mix wants to continue rising after the crust is set. Placing the dish low in the oven stops the crust setting and browning before the heat has penetrated the interior. The variable cooking time allows for variation in the surface area of the dish: the wider and shallower the dish the shorter the baking time. In the garlic soufflé recipe (see p. 104) a soufflé twice this size in a shallow oval dish measuring 12 in (30 cm) long by 2 in (5 cm) deep takes but 10 minutes at 230°/450°F/ Gas Mark 8.

Changing the ingredients

Use celery salt instead of salt and add fresh or dried sage to taste.

The following flavour variations involve the addition of extra ingredients to the basic recipe. This will make the soufflés heavier but good all the same.

Add 6 oz (170 g) cooked, chopped spinach, warmed in 1 oz (30 g) of browned garlicky butter, to the cheesy béchamel. This soufflé, served with a pourable anchovy- or Parma ham-flavoured cream, makes an exciting starter.

Replace the spinach with aubergine chopped to pea size, fried brown in garlic oil and butter until soft, then drained. Add a dessertspoon of chopped fresh coriander.

Replace the spinach with a celeriac purée made from young celeriac, poached in its skin (a microwave poaches celeriac splendidly). Halve the amount of cheese. This variation makes an exotic side dish to roast lamb.

Other side-dish partnerships include a soufflé flavoured with cooked fennel purée, brightened with a splash of Pernod and a few fennel seeds, to accompany grilled gammon; and one flavoured with puréed parsnips and a grate or two of fresh horseradish, which is a perfect match to a game stew.

Season all these vegetable soufflés well, their flavours are much diminished when cooked.

See also recipes for oyster soufflé and garlic soufflé (p. 104).

Raspberry soufflé

Serves 6
$\frac{3}{4}$ lb (340 g) fresh or frozen raspberries
$5\frac{1}{4}$ oz (150 g) icing sugar
1 or two teaspoons lemon juice
3 egg yolks
12 egg whites

Blend the raspberries with 3 oz (85 g) of icing sugar and the lemon juice. You can sieve out the seeds from the resulting purée if you like smoothness. Beat the yolks until pale and stir into the mix.

Butter 6 ramekins, size 4×2 in (10×5 cm). Put some caster sugar into these well-buttered ramekins, shake about until all buttered surfaces are coated and tip out the surplus.

Beat the egg whites to soft peaks and, near the end of the beating, sprinkle in $2\frac{1}{4}$ oz (65 g) of icing sugar while the beating continues.

Stir a quarter of the whites into the raspberry purée then lightly fold in the rest. Fill the ramekins to the brim and level off with a straight edge. Push the mixture away from the edges with your thumb.

Place in the middle of the oven at 220°C/400°F/Gas Mark 6 for 12 minutes. Sieve a little icing sugar onto the top of the soufflé some 3 minutes into the cooking time and remember to close the oven door gently: a slammed door creates compression in the oven depressing the tender blooming of the soufflé.

This recipe is so light in texture that it will need some succulence. An apricot sauce is nice but I prefer lightly whipped, sweetened cream flavoured with quality framboise or kirsch liqueur.

How the recipe works

The sugar lining in the ramekins is for texture, and pushing the mixture away from the edges will stop the skin, as it forms, from sticking to the sides and holding down the expansion.

A dusting of icing sugar gives a professional brown sheen to the crust.

Changing the ingredients

The purée technique also works well with savoury combinations: puréed smoked fish or ham are good as a light main course and vegetable purées make tasty light soufflés, but it is a clever cook who can fit a meal around them as a main course. They are perfect for a side dish, however; see above (p. 47).

All of the following variations should be sweetened to taste, bearing in mind that the finished soufflés will seem less sweet than the purée. The quantity of purée needed will be about the same as for the basic recipe.

Instead of raspberries use a purée made from the following alternatives: dried apricots softened with sweet white wine, made curiously interesting with a pinch of mace; prunes with rum and a pinch of salt; fresh ripe pears spiked with pear-flavoured liqueur (be quick, naked fresh pear turns brown frighteningly quickly); or fresh or frozen red currants, adding a few whole currants to the mixture just before filling the ramekins.

The accompanying sauce needed for these very light soufflés can be compatibly flavoured cream, as in the basic recipe, or one made from the purée used in the recipe diluted with an appropriately flavoured alcohol. A pinch of fresh-chopped mint will add a little mystery if you are feeling adventurous.

Delicious lemon pudding

Serves 4
2 oz (55 g) salted butter
7 oz (200 g) sugar
1 oz (30 g) self-raising flour
1 lemon
2 eggs
5 fl oz (140 ml) milk

Blend or cream the butter and sugar. Add the flour, the juice and grated zest of the lemon and the egg yolks. Add the milk and gently beaten egg whites. Pour the semi-liquid into a buttered soufflé dish large enough to be filled three quarters full.

Stand in a baking tray in $\frac{1}{2}$ in (1.5 cm) of water and put into a moderate oven (set midway along the dial) for 45 minutes.

As with the soufflés this recipe works well in small ramekins, this quantity yielding 5 small puddings with nicely browned tops in about 10–12 minutes in a hot oven (200°C/400°F/Gas Mark 6).

How the recipe works

The blending of the sugar with the butter shows that this dish was devised by a pudding and cake cook (almost all cake recipes start that way). The slackness of the final mix enables the whites to expand easily and, like the soufflé it so nearly is, to collapse as easily.

The water in the tray prevents the mixture from drying out in the bottom of the dish, as well as providing humidity in the oven. This yields the tenderest, moist, sponge texture wherein lies its ephemeral charm, reminiscent as it is of a freshly baked sponge hot from the oven.

The unset mixture at the bottom, protected from the heat by the water, has a stronger-than-you-would-have-thought lemon taste, rather like lemon curd with a little flour added. This is far from unpleasant, reminding the more fortunate among us of childhood hours hanging around the kitchen waiting to lick the cake mixing bowl. Even without that memory, this floury taste is a fine balance to the cooked sponge expanded above it. All that is needed to provide a memorable experience is some good whipping cream.

On occasions, I introduce half a capful of lemon gin into each ramekin before filling. Lemon gin is to be had from Amsterdam or from grated lemon zest suspended in slightly sweetened London gin. Gin on its own isn't bad either.

Boiling and Steaming

The transfer of heat to food by hot liquid or steam is probably the simplest and safest technique for the budding cook to master. Apart from the effect of altitude or atmospheric pressure, of which more later, the temperature of boiling water is constant at 100°C (212°F) and that of steam a degree or two above that. It follows then that cooking times with it are consistent, making it a simpler medium to master than others. With such low top temperatures, these techniques can't produce the browning that adds so much to the flavour-making process, and hence the association of boiling and steaming with blandness.

Vegetables

There is a distinction to be made as to which vegetables should be boiled and which steamed. Some, like Brussels sprouts, cabbage, chicory and asparagus, benefit from losing a little of their bitterness and are better boiled. Others – especially those with a more delicate flavour like broccoli, peas and young root vegetables such as carrots and parsnips – lose less flavour when steamed.

Vegetables can keep most of their flavour, brilliance and vitamin content if cooked with the following good rules in mind. (Asparagus is a special case, and advice on cooking it can be found on p. 125.)

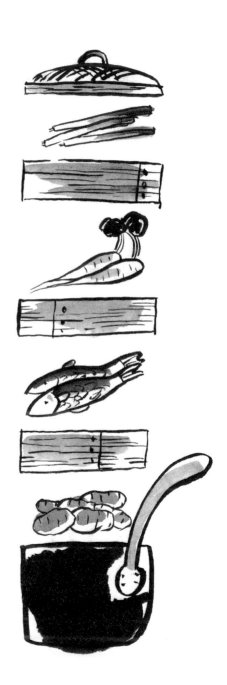

Preparation

Cut up the vegetables as near to the cooking time as possible. Enzymes in the structure of vegetables are released by cutting and these attack both vitamins and colour.

Cut vegetables into regular bite-sized pieces so that they cook in minimal time. Shortening the fibre effectively tenderizes food, so cut the coarser parts of the vegetables – the stalks usually – into thin slices across the grain, shortening the fibre and increasing the surface area exposed to heat. Or keep these tougher bits apart and put them into the pan first for extra cooking before adding more tender pieces.

Cooking

Put the vegetables into plenty of fast boiling water. This cuts the time the water goes off the boil when cold vegetables are put in. This is critical as the temperature for maximum loss of chlorophyll is below boiling point at 66–77°C (150°-170°F).

Cook green vegetables with the lid off the pan. Vegetables give off chlorophyll-attacking acids during the first 2–3 minutes of boiling. They vaporize with the steam. 'Vegetables that grow in the open like to cook in the open' said one good cook I used to know.

Chlorophyll can be affected in other ways. Hard water makes vegetables turn mushy and this allows green chlorophyll to leach away. Soft water changes the chemical nature of chlorophyll and its colour. Either way colour is lost. Soft water with added salt is the best bet to keep the colour.

Altitude and pressure cooking

Water boils at 100°C (212°F) at sea level, but the higher the altitude, the lower the boiling point of water and the longer vegetables take to cook in it. And since the time that vegetables are exposed to heat is in direct ratio to loss of colour and vitamins, it follows that boiling them in a kitchen half way up a mountain could have a depressing result – unless you have a pressure cooker.

This pan, with its screw-down lid and weights to hold in the steam, can raise the temperature of boiling up to 120°C (248°F) so it can solve the altitude problem. At this super-heat, food cooks so fast that colour and vitamin loss is kept to a minimum. In spite of this advantage, pressure cooking isn't popular even at altitude. As it reaches high pressure, steam escapes from the cooker through its safety valve accompanied by much hissing, and this frightens timid cooks who expect that at any minute it is about to explode. It stops being so menacing once it is realised that hissing is a sign that the safety valve is working and that silence, while boiling, is a sign of danger.

Pressure cooking's speed really counts when cooking meat stews or chickpeas – these cook in less than half the normal cooking time – but as usual something has to be paid for this advantage. The business of getting the lid off the pan, to see how things are going, requires getting the pressure down and that means putting it for a time under a cold tap. After a couple of such coolings, with the attendant hissing and spluttering, some of the time saved is lost along with one's admiration for the process. Nor is its speed a great advantage when cooking delicate food – green vegetables, for instance, are cooked in seconds rather than minutes. Even so, with a second timer, it is possible to produce attractively green, vitamin-rich, nicely cooked vegetables in it – and not only up a mountain.

Blanching

Much used in professional kitchens, blanching is where green vegetables are pre-boiled in such a way as to cut the final cooking to a minimum and limit the loss of chlorophyll green when the vegetables are reheated. Rapid heating to 100°C (212°F) kills the enzyme responsible for changing the nature of chlorophyll, thus fixing the colour, so to speak.

Good blanching needs plenty of boiling water with plenty of salt (half as much again as you would normally use), which raises the boiling point and speeds the cooking time. When green vegetables are plunged into this salty cauldron, they will turn a more vivid green almost immediately, because the surface layer, which refracts a lot of light, becomes tender and then collapses to reveal the chlorophyll-green flesh lying underneath.

Boil the vegetables for only a third of the usual cooking time, then strain and cool them as quickly as possible – putting them under a running cold tap is the usual method. With normal cooking times, such a quantity of salt would make the vegetables inedible, but, since they are in salt water for a short time and in unsalted water until they are cold, they lose most of the salt they have absorbed. Blanched vegetables are reheated by plunging them into boiling water for a minute, by stir-frying or by giving them a quick flick in the microwave.

Blanching isn't a particularly good way of preserving vitamins, but it is an excellent way of reheating vegetables and keeping them green at the same time. The old-fashioned way, by putting bicarbonate of soda in the cooking water, does preserve the green too but it makes the vegetables mushy and changes the taste for the worse.

Vitamin C

In a healthy diet with plenty of fresh food, vitamin loss through cooking hardly matters, but psychologically it is always worth saving what vitamins you can, even if you don't specifically need them at the moment. Vitamin C in vegetables is lost in several ways; it dissolves in water; it is attacked by enzymes present in the flesh of plants when they are released from the cell structure by cutting; and it can be destroyed by heat and by long exposure to air.

When vegetables are boiled, they lose more vitamin C in the boiling water than they would if steamed. Vitamin C is leached out during boiling but other acids, also present in the cell structure, are as well. As mentioned earlier, these acids attack chlorophyll so that boiled greens stand to keep their colour (once the acids have been diluted) but lose their vitamins. Conversely, steamed greens keep their chlorophyll-attacking acid as well as their vitamins.

All seems clear then: when deciding between steaming or boiling greens you choose between your health or the appearance of the food. Would that it were so simple. The enzymes I mentioned above attack vitamins most actively between 60° and 80°C (140–175°F) and are finally destroyed at 100°C (212°F). They are water soluble too and are leached out with the vitamins in boiling water, evaporating with the steam if the lid is left off the pan. In steaming they continue to attack the vitamins, especially before the vegetable reaches 100°C (212°F). But microwaving (of which more later) is much faster than either; the loss by heat is less and the enzymes have little chance of destroying vitamins in so short a time – no wonder the flavour seems superior.

Flavour

Adding extra flavour to good fresh vegetables would seem like gilding the lily, but when their flavours are familiar, which they become if you have a gardenful, the intriguing surprise element that keeps attention on the food is soon lost. Cooking vegetables with other flavours in the water is one way of reviving that surprise element, and it works wonders with jaded vegetables too.

The well-known affinity of mint with peas or new potatoes shows how well the practice works, but that is only the beginning. Fresh coriander is magic with green beans or courgettes (add a whole sprig or two to the cooking water, just as you would add mint to peas), as is orange zest with carrots, dill (quite a lot of it) with spinach, caraway with green, red or white cabbage, tarragon with cauliflower, basil with okra or tomatoes and fresh chilli with parsnips. This is a great area for experimenting.

Pulses

The time taken to cook these satisfying vegetables varies enormously according to age, size and whether the cellular skin has been split from them or not. Perhaps the safest way of getting them soft but whole is to leave them to soak until reconstituted (overnight always seems a convenient time); then cook, testing as you do so, until they are soft. Chickpeas, marrowfat peas or really old pulses take the devil of a time to soften even when soaked. Old fashioned cooks used soda to hasten the process which gave them an odd, but not altogether unpleasant, flavour at the same time. Since the advent of the speedy pressure cooker, this adulteration is no longer necessary.

Flatulence

Dried peas and beans contain a chemical, oligosaccharide, which is indigestible to human digestive enzymes but tractable to the bacteria in the intestine. In the course of digesting this chemical, the latter produce the malodorous gases and flatulence that give pulses such a bad name. Cooking in boiling water with the lid off certainly helps to remove some of the offensive chemical. I boil pulses in plenty of water, change the water after a 5-minute boil without a lid and only add salt when they are soft, since salt seems to inhibit the softening.

Fish

The flesh of fish is made of flakes of short-grain protein fibre held together with gelatinous connecting tissue. When this tissue becomes softened, as it does in hot water, the flakes become loose. If fish is boiled rapidly the turbulence of the water will soon start to break it up. It is wise then to poach or steam fish and not boil it unless a chowder is planned.

I poach fish by immersing it in just enough boiling fish stock to cover; when the liquid has returned to the boil, I keep the surface of it barely smiling – not even a simmer – for a few minutes only, before turning off the heat altogether and letting the residual heat in the stock finish the job. I prefer this to steaming as it allows a good flavoured stock to add its resonance to the fish.

Meat and Poultry

These don't have the short grain that fish has and with longer fibres they hold together for much longer, even in turbulent conditions. The tougher the cut of meat or boiling fowl, the tastier the end result. The reason for this seems to lie in the amount of collagen (i.e. sinew and gristle) holding the muscles together. When collagen is boiled, it dissolves into a gelatinous gravy producing a delicious all-round-the-mouth succulence. It takes a long simmer to tenderize the collagen, during which time the muscle fibres have given up their juiciness and become quite crumbly and shrunken, but this is part and parcel of making a stew with a rich gravy, even with the slowest cooking. The meat's tasty juiciness is traded for a tasty gravy with dessicated lumps of meat.

It is possible to get the best of both worlds and have tasty gravy and juicy meat. Make a succulent stock of the coarse-fibred meat and discard them, or chop them into very small pieces so that their dryness becomes imperceptible. Then add the tender bits, suitably cut fine across the grain, for the last few minutes of cooking time.

With poultry, use the carcass and drumsticks, with some pot herbs, for the gravy and, when strained, add the sliced breasts and thigh meat with some diced raw pot herbs (onions, carrots, celery, etc.) for just a minute or two. The meat will be juicy, the pot herbs will be bright and crunchy and the gravy rich – a magical combination.

Stocks and Soups

Stock is made from boiling food until all or most of its flavour has been given to the water. There are two kinds. One is made quickly with fresh herbs and vegetables as the flavouring. This is light and fragrant, enhancing delicately flavoured food, which a stronger stock might drown. This light kind of stock is particularly suited to fish, but it can enliven rather bland vegetables like vegetable marrow or chard. Chard looks so very promising, like a thick, white-stemmed spinach, but has a flavour so

delicate as to be almost imperceptible, while vegetable marrow is like a chameleon, taking protective flavour from the closest taste to hand. Both improve mightily when poached in a fresh vegetable stock.

The other kind of stock is more familiar. It is made with bones and gristle but it lacks piquancy unless perfumed with vegetables, herbs, spices and seasoning. There is a danger that the individual flavour of the bones will gradually disappear with prolonged simmering until all that is left is a general all-round-the-mouth taste, well on its way to being glue. This anonymous fate can overtake any stock that has been over-reduced. See recipes on pp. 94–5.

Consommé

A good consommé is a well-flavoured stock, gently reduced so that the identity of its source material is strengthened, and clarified. The flavour should have a hint of acidity and a little *umami*.

Reduce the stock (see pp. 94–5 for recipes) with fresh vegetables and herbs, especially if the flavour seems a bit flaccid, and adjust the seasoning before clarifying. Strain the stock through a fine sieve and chill.

When the stock has gelled, turn it out of its container and cut off the sediment from the bottom and the fat from the top. Warm the stock and stir in lightly beaten egg-whites (2 whites to 3 pints/1.7 litres of stock). Bring it to the gentlest of simmers – as someone said 'let the surface smile not laugh' – stirring all the time for ten minutes. Let the stock settle, off the heat, for another ten minutes. The whites will have set, catching most if not all of the remaining sediment. Strain the stock through the sieve – this time lined with a fine muslin cloth – leaving the whites behind in the cloth and a crystal clear consommé in the pan.

Rarely does a consommé have enough character to stand completely on its own and one way to lift the flavour is to add alcohol. Sherry or Madeira enhance rich game consommé (1 tablespoon per pint/570 ml) and dryish white wine does the same for fish and chicken dishes (experiment with a sample before treating the whole amount).

It is also usual to have something to chew on while the soup is drunk. This is sound practice as chewing increases the saliva flow, which in turn heightens the flavour. I use raw firm vegetables cut in minute cubes and put these in the soup bowl before filling them with soup. Carrots, firm tomato flesh, watercress leaves, chopped fresh herb stalks or a little fine-chopped chilli or capsicum are all very suitable. Nor should something sharp be overlooked, if further enhancement is needed. Try lemon juice, tabasco, Worcestershire sauce or mushroom relish – sometimes just a drop or two will do the trick.

Thicker soups

All the enhancing tricks used on consommé work with thicker soups too. For example, supping a creamed tomato soup with soft bread is nowhere near as satisfying as supping it with crisp toast or crunchy croutons. If croutons are added to the soup, better make them fried as these are the most water-proof. See p. 142 for a garlic crouton recipe. For other ideas on soup recipes, see pp. 96–101.

Puddings

Steamed puddings are instant nostalgia. It is understandable: sweet, moist, filling and warm, they are a child's idea of ambrosia. Of the myriad recipes to choose from, I have picked one for the recipe chapter, Alexander pudding (see p. 142), which makes splendid small individual puddings. They freeze like a dream, so if you have a supply in your freezer, and a microwave, home-made puddings can be served almost at the drop of a hat. The recipe uses fresh breadcrumbs, which make light sponges that are not temperamental, and their flavour, a sort of unboiled fresh marmalade, marries nicely with an honest, lemony-egg custard sauce. This nursery food de luxe can be made adult with a slurp of orange liqueur.

Eggs

Put an egg in water to see if it is fresh. Very fresh eggs sink fairly quickly, while staler eggs float with the broad end higher than the narrow.

Once the shell is broken, the difference between a fresh and stale egg is clearly visible.

A fresh egg has two sorts of egg white: a thicker white (or albumen) which holds together around the yolk and a thinner white which falls away and lies like a puddle. As the egg gets staler, the thicker white gradually dissolves into the thin until no albumen at all protects the yolk.

The yolk tells a tale too: the rounder it is, the fresher the egg. Stale yolks have weaker membranes holding them together, so, like a slack balloon, they lie flatter and are easily broken.

Soft-boiled eggs

A gourmet uncle of mine, whose opinion I respected, once told me that you could always tell a good hotel from an indifferent one by the state of their boiled eggs. I smiled at the time, but when starting my own hotel I took good care to see that, with boiled eggs at least, we would make the grade. A perfect soft-boiled egg, with a set but not hard white and a runny yolk, continues to cook in its own heat once out of boiling water and stands a good chance of being beyond its best if not consumed straight away. With talkative guests this is a

distinct possibility, so, to safeguard against this, we used to put it in cold water for 15–20 seconds after cooking.

To boil an egg, put it in a pan with plenty of boiling water. Lower it in with a spoon to stop it bumping the bottom and cracking the shell. Have the egg near room temperature – an egg straight from the fridge is more likely to crack when plunged into boiling water. Commence timing when the water starts to boil again. For a medium size egg allow 3 minutes 20 seconds at sea level, and then, if it is not to be eaten immediately give it a cold water douche. For a large egg allow 4 minutes.

Hard-boiled eggs

Fresh hard-boiled eggs are harder to shell than stale. When fresh, egg whites have distinct layers, as already explained, and the outermost layer of thin albumen easily parts from the inner, thicker layer and sticks to the shell membrane instead, leaving a far from smooth shape. In staler eggs these layers become one, which, when set, is quite robust enough to hold a smooth egg shape. A fresh hard-boiled egg will have its yolk in the middle of the white, while in a stale one the yolk can be seen from the outside because the thicker albumen has dissolved and no longer holds the yolk away from the shell.

When an egg is over-boiled, the prolonged exposure to heat gives the yolk an unsightly greeny-grey surface. Avoid this by boiling only just enough to set the yolk hard (about 7 or 8 minutes) then plunge it into cold water immediately. Shell the egg as soon as it is cool enough to handle – it is easier to do then – and return it to cold water until quite cold.

Poached eggs

These are eggs that are boiled – or, properly speaking, simmered – without their shells.

Break an egg into a cup and slide it into a pan of simmering water – well, to be exact, the water should be taken off the boil before sliding the egg into it. There should be enough water to cover the egg. Once the outside of the egg white is set, return the water to a simmer then remove the pan from the heat. Leave the egg to poach for about $3\frac{1}{2}$ minutes and remove it with a slotted spoon, letting the water drain away. I usually break away some of the more untidy white for appearance's sake.

If the egg in the cup looks stale (see above), put salt or lemon juice into the water, as this holds the albumen together better.

Scrambled eggs

These are eggs which have been beaten before cooking, and they are heated gently, without water, in a pan until they are just set. For perfection, they should be creamy and moist when served. Just like boiled eggs, they continue to cook in their own heat so it is better to reduce the rate of heating once coagulation begins. Scrambled eggs become crumbly if overcooked, but they can be rescued with a raw egg

yolk stirred in with a little cream – gently reheat if the curds look a bit raw. If the rate of cooking is reduced to a crawl, once cooked, they can be held warm for quite a while – say 15 minutes. One of the tricks with scrambled eggs is to add cream, about 2–3 teaspoons per egg, to the beaten eggs to add succulence and keep the finished dish lighter.

These are conventional scrambled eggs, but see p. 107 for the lighter, microwaving way.

Frying

The frying medium, oil or fat, is a good conductor of heat, making this technique potentially faster than other conventional techniques. This speed makes it possible to get a brown, crisp surface on food while leaving the interior almost uncooked – very convenient when cooking fish fillets or other thin foods. Since browning is flavour-enhancing and so easy to get with frying, it is often employed as a first stage when stewing or braising. 'Brown the onions and meat in a frying pan' is a typical beginning to such recipes.

Frying is commonly divided into categories according to the amount of oil or fat used. In *deep-frying*, food is completely immersed in oil; in *sautéing*, or *shallow-* or *pan-frying*, a film of oil lubricates the frying pan, coating and cooking the bottom of food only; in *stir-frying*, a similar amount of oil is used but food is coated and cooked on all sides by continual stirring; and in *searing*, a smear of oil in the pan is allowed to burn onto food for the special flavour it gives.

Frying is the only process where the cooking medium adds flavour to food, so a word on oil or fat won't be out of place.

Fats

The effect of using refined fat rather than oil lies more in the difference in melting point than any real difference in actual frying quality. Emulsified oils (by which I mean modern, solid, vegetable fats) are refined to death to extend their shelf life and remove objectionable odours, and they have little flavour to add to food apart from a slight twang in the aftertaste after frying.

Unrefined oil or fat is quite a different matter. Happy the cook who roasts meat or poultry regularly and has plenty of flavourful fat to hand. Use the dripping from roast beef, the lard from pork or the fat from a chicken to pan-fry potatoes – the flavour these fats give really can't be beaten – and use unrefined dripping or lard when making pastry for the extra richness it gives to savoury pies. More unconventionally, use it in the pastry for sweet, sharp fruit pies – it gives a sensational old-fashioned flavour.

Butter is excellent for frying and good for *umami*, the all-round fifth taste, but the milk solids in it burn while the food being fried starts to brown, these black specks are bitter and spoil the look of food too. Overcome this

by clarifying the butter – that is melting it. The milk solids settle to the bottom, leaving a clear butter fat to pour off and use for frying. Keep the curds to add later when they won't burn or use them to make a noisette.

Noisette

This excellent nutty-flavoured butter sauce is made from butter curds and any residual fat left behind with the curds when clarifying butter. Fry the curds gently until they are pale brown and add this, sizzling, to a dish just before serving. Noisette, sharpened with lemon juice and colour-contrasted with chopped green herb, is the sauce used for the famous Dover sole à la meunière (see p. 111). Noisette is delicious added to a warm vinaigrette on hot vegetables like asparagus. When making hollandaise, think about clarifying the butter (it has to be melted anyway) and browning the curds before adding them to the sauce.

Oils

Apart from the highly refined commercial oils – sunflower, soya, rape-seed and the like – there are others that aren't so shy in adding flavour. Cooking-quality olive oil leaves a detectable flavour, as do the oils produced from peanuts or sesame seeds which have been toasted beforehand. This toasting gives the oil a pronounced nutty flavour and a light caramel colour, and I use them to add flavour towards

the end of frying. Toasting shortens the keeping quality of these oils and it is prudent to keep them, well corked, in a fridge. Quality nut oils, like walnut or hazelnut, should really be kept for salads or as a dressing for hot vegetables, since they are expensive and burn bitter very easily.

Cooking oil deteriorates when heated. Kept at frying temperature for hours at a time, it ages faster and, when overheated to smoking point, faster still. This hardly matters with sautéing or stir-frying, as almost no oil is left in the pan to be used again, but with deep-frying, most of the oil is re-used many times until, in poorly run restaurants, it almost turns to varnish. There are clear signs to tell you when your oil is going stale: it takes longer to brown food, it starts to froth rather than bubble and it begins to smell rank rather than sweet – all these are sure signs that its cooking hours are over. The smell of stale cooking oil when you enter a restaurant will tell you all you need to know about the chef, the manager and the dyspepsia that is likely to follow if you eat there.

Deep-Frying

Of all the ways of frying this is the one that gets food the crispest, and that is its main attraction, for crispness, as every potato crisp manufacturer knows, is compelling. Deep-fried potatoes, chips or french fries are everywhere, and the crisper they are fried the more compulsive they become. Crispness has much to do with the size of the potato chip being fried. All chips leave the oil with a crisp browned surface but thicker ones still have enough moisture inside to soften the surface after a time, while thin chips, with their centres less moist, stay crisper longer.

Apart from crisp-frying the ubiquitous chip, deep-frying is the easiest and really the only way to fry doughnuts or anything dipped in batter or wrapped in filo pastry. It is also the best way to crisp-fry small fishes and slivers of meat to a crunchy brown. In spite of this, deep-frying is not much used in my kitchen since it is wasteful of oil – it would be scandalous to use my well-flavoured fats this way. Nor does its lingering smell endear it either. This may have something to do with my kitchen and dining table being in the same room. I'd use it more if the arrangements were different but I'm not prepared to sacrifice the joy of company while cooking for the sake of a crisp chip. On the assumption that you are of like mind I'll leave it to others and the manuals that come with a deep-fryer to explain the intricacies of the technique. If deep-frying is essential I use a wok. It means frying in small quantity, so the number to dine will be restricted accordingly, and the menu planned with care to allow enough time for it.

Sautéing (Shallow-Frying or Pan-Frying)

Fish

The problem with sautéing fish is that it tends to stick to the pan while being fried. With deep-frying, the coating – be it batter or breadcrumb – seals the fish in a uniform protection which makes it easy to handle and keep whole. With stir-frying, individual pieces, tossed as

they are, hardly have time to stick to the wok. But with sautéing, the fish is static and sometimes sticks to the pan as it is cooking. The traditional way of avoiding disaster, as well as giving an attractive browning, is to dry the fish and coat it with flour before frying. This does help, but the body fluids, released by the heat of the pan, act like glue, with or without flour. The problem is accentuated by the wetness of the fish.

There is no foolproof answer. A well-seasoned pan with enough really hot oil to give an initial browning before finishing the cooking in an oven is one way of getting round the problem.

Meat and chicken

The speed of frying doesn't give time for connecting tissue and gristle in meat to soften before the muscle is cooked, so only gristle-free meat is suitable unless it is cut small enough to be swallowed easily. Any cut of meat that can be grilled can be fried with equal success. Where the speed of frying really works is with thinner cuts, but even then, if juiciness is to be preserved, you'll have to be quick about it. With something really thin like a slice of veal cut for a schnitzel, by the time the escalope has fried brown on one side, it is almost cooked through, and to brown the other side would be to overcook it. The way I deal with this is to sear the second side quickly and leave it at that. The nicely browned side is uppermost when served of course.

Vegetables

These brown very nicely in a pan with only a smear of oil. This method can be used to brown onions and other pot herbs, so that a good brown Maillard taste can be given to a stew which it couldn't get by boiling alone. This use of pan-frying, while not doing much for green vegetables, does lend considerable charm to tomatoes and red peppers. It seems to have something to do with the cut edge of the skin and the interaction of the browning with the juices that are drying and mingling with the fat.

To fry a tomato, cut it in half and place it, face down, in a lightly greased pan on medium heat. After a while the edges of the skin start to take colour and, if left for long enough, eventually turn chocolate brown. The flavour build-up is intense – almost salty, certainly a little bitter (as the sugar in the tomato caramelizes) and this quite transforms a bland commercial tomato. The skins of red peppers benefit from this treatment too (see p. 129).

I hesitate to talk of frying potatoes, but do try my current method given on pp. 129–130, it is so good. The recipe calls for a microwave to soften the potatoes but they can be par-boiled if you don't have one.

Pancakes

The sort of pancakes that you fry will depend, as much as anything, on the style of batter made and how suitable the pans are. Yes, I said pans in the plural, for unless you fancy standing like a dumpling for hours by a hot stove, the art of making pancakes quickly will have to be mastered, and for that you need two frying pans. No matter if one is bigger than the other, much more important is how well they are seasoned. A seasoned pan will allow pancakes, once nicely browned on one side, to detach themselves and slide about if the pan is given a quick jerk backwards and forwards. Some batters are self-lubricating – they have oil or melted butter in their recipe – and this speeds production, since otherwise the pans need greasing between each pancake.

If you have different-sized pans, use the smaller of the two to govern the size of the pancake – a pan about 6–8 in (15–20 cm) in diameter is a useful size. Into this well-greased pan, hot enough to make a drop of water sizzle and jump about, pour a measured amount of batter. A ladle will make it easier to judge the quantity of batter and give a consistent thickness to each pancake. Once the pancake is brown and detached, flick it over into the other pan, also hot and greasy, to brown the other side. Reckon to lose a few pancakes while you adjust the thickness of the batter, the greasiness of the pan and the heat, which will govern the pace of production.

Once you have developed a rhythm and nicely browned pancakes are flowing off the range, it is easy to fry off another batch for freezing, placing a layer of cling film between each pancake. To resuscitate the pancakes straight from the freezer, re-fry on the first side only. This should defrost them and restore the crispness that freshly made pancakes have. This re-frying is so quick that you can contemplate having pancakes as a course at a dinner. Recipes for several sorts of pancake are to be found on pp. 102–4.

Stir-Frying

This is the half-way house between pan-frying and searing. Tenderize pieces of food by cutting them small across the grain and then half-fry or half-sear them with a little oil in a very hot and smoky pan. This needs to be large enough to allow for the frantic stirring around needed to prevent small pieces of food from sticking. The idea is to burn the edges of the pieces, which have been cut small enough to be par-cooked by the time this has happened. Softening and overcooking is the big danger, as once juice from the food is released, stir-frying turns into boiling.

Most domestic ranges are nowhere near bold enough for a wok, unable to deliver anywhere near the intensity of heat needed. If you're lucky enough to own a gas cooker, I suggest that you remove the spreader from the largest ring to get a decent plume of flame to lick around the wok. Apart from that, the best method is to forget all about a wok and use your heaviest pan as hot as you dare. Whatever happens don't put in so much food that the temperature drops and the food simmers rather than sizzles. Better to sear a small amount and leave it to cook in its own heat elsewhere while you get on with the next lot. Once all the ingredients have had a fry-up, drain the juices from this steaming pile of food back into the pan; then, adding whatever extra flavouring you've decided to use, reduce the liquid to a tasty sauce and roll the warm food in it.

Microwaving

All traditional methods of cooking heat the surface of food only, relying on water, present to a greater or lesser extent in most food, to conduct the heat generated on the surface to the interior. With microwaving, sub-infra-red waves vibrate food molecules, causing them to rub against each other and create heat, not only on the surface but penetrating into food to a depth of an inch or so all round. All

molecules that are polar get vibrated but air, glass, plastic and most forms of crockery, being non-polar, stay cool. You can tell which crockery is affected by microwaving it for a few seconds. If it stays cool, you can use it. Any sound of crackling or sparks flying in the oven suggests the presence of metal, which, if ignored, can wreck it.

All food molecules get vibrated, but three sets – water, fat, and sugar – seem particularly affected. Water molecules, excited to boiling point, produce steam which cooks food in a micro very much as if it were being steamed in a traditional way but considerably faster. Fat molecules, when excited, heat up to a higher temperature than water, so that they fry in their own heat. Any spitting that happens comes from water molecules trapped in the fat,

which expand explosively into steam as they boil. Sugar molecules, when excited, get so hot they caramelize.

As with any cooking process, microwaving has its pros and cons. To my mind, it should be regarded as an extremely useful, economic, speedy, new (and therefore suspect) tool, which can cook any food that can be stewed or boiled quicker and better than conventional methods.

Limitations

Calling the microwave an oven is a misnomer since it cannot roast or bake as we understand it. To produce browning, as on the outside of a roast joint, the surface of food has to be free from water. But microwaves heat the interior of food at the same time as the surface, so that when the surface is dry enough to brown, the interior will be dried out too.

On the whole, microwaving doesn't excel at cooking large pieces of meat or poultry, and I prefer to roast them in a conventional oven and use the micro as a safety net. An undercooked roast from a conventional oven, for example, can be rescued by microwaving pieces cut from it. These pieces should be fairly regular in shape – thin or narrow parts tend to get over-cooked. The microwaving has to be done with care – seconds rather than minutes – but then, when these pieces are carved, it is hard to tell that the roast hasn't had its full time in the conventional oven.

The microwave is poor with other food normally baked in an oven. I've had no success with making soufflés, breads or, despite manufacturer's claims, cakes.

Strengths

The real magic of the process lies in steaming, especially fish, vegetables and fruit; in stewing, especially meat that has gristle in it (it has a nifty way of converting gristle to gelatin faster than traditional cooking); in reheating, where it is way ahead of any other process in the speed and the freshness of the result; in making sauces, which would thicken and burn on an ordinary stove unless stirred constantly (not so much a triumph for the microwave process as for the switching gear which allows limited bursts of full power, interspersed with pauses while the heat disseminates throughout); in saving the washing up of those burnt sauce-pans; and in browning nuts, caramelizing sugar, melting chocolate and butter. It is also a life-saver for the absent-minded because of its ability to defrost food quickly, although I'm not too happy about the irregularity of the defrosting – exposed parts tend to cook rather than defrost – and much prefer to allow it to take place more naturally.

Microwaving can do curious things to flavours, accentuating some and depressing others. I usually flavour with caution before microwaving and adjust the flavour afterwards. Beware of nutmeg, mace, ginger powder, pepper, cinnamon and dried herbs which seem to get accentuated, while others like coriander, caraway and cumin seeds, garlic and fresh herbs seem to weaken.

Microwaving, being a novel process, has attracted much uninformed opinion about its abilities. There was the apocryphal story of the lady who popped her dog in the micro to dry its hair. A more serious charge is the murderous effect a microwave is supposed to have on vitamins. On this point the knowledgeable Harold McGee says that exposure to heat from any source, be it of a traditional nature or microwaving, will cause the water-soluble vitamins C and B to deteriorate. Speedy cooking preserves them more, and with vitamin C in particular, the crucial temperature at which enzymes attack vitamin C is kept to a minimum. Finally, vitamins A and C are water soluble and microwaves need very little water, or none at all, to steam efficiently. It must be at least arguable that microwaving saves more vitamins than any other cooking technique.

Over the years, I have found microwaves to be pretty well indispensable. Certainly they are a valuable asset in making the impossible possible and there are things that can't be cooked any other way. Unfortunately it is the microwave's talent to heat or, more particularly, reheat food that causes many problems. The microwave makes it possible to serve good hot food at table as if it has just been prepared, and this allows factory-prepared food to be passed as on-site cooking. Anyone who knows the limitations of the process will probably be able to detect when micros are about anyway. There are giveaways that help. Mic-rowaving produces steam and this will slacken the crisp surface of fried and baked foods. Food that has been microwaved carries on heating up after cooking, so that a dish that arrives steaming hot on a table probably indicates that there is a micro in the kitchen.

Some eaters claim that they can detect any food that has been microwaved because it gives a slightly 'off' taste. This may be right but most people can't or don't notice this, and I suspect that it is only possible when food has been overcooked rather than treated with the respect that such a powerful tool demands.

The defence of the microwave can go on, but with the late lamented Jane Grigson as a convert, I feel that the case can rest with her words on the subject in the *Observer* (1/10/89): 'Sceptical readers, unconvinced by this late conversion, can stop raising their eyebrows or blowing on their glasses. In my articles, I shall stick to classic methods in the recipes, knowing that anyone with a microwave will be smart enough to use it for shortcuts that improve the final result without my telling them.'

Cooking uses

Baked potatoes

Almost the first use to which people put their microwaves is to make 'baked' potatoes. It saves an impressive amount of cooking time, reducing it from at least an hour to about five minutes. But the real charm of a baked potato lies in the dried brown skin, which is beyond the power of a microwave. The scorched flavour and the chewy texture contrast wonderfully with the mealy inside, but for the skin to acquire this particular charm requires a good twenty minutes in a hot oven. The micro can at least speed the cooking of the inside.

Turn the conventional oven on high at the start of proceedings and, by the time it is hot, the potatoes will be cooked through in the microwave. Put the softened potatoes onto the top shelf of the hot oven, which then only needs to dry out the skin to get the desirable brown crust – about thirty minutes from start to finish.

Scrambled eggs

This simple dish is hardly one that needs a micro to produce it, but the advantage of not having scrambled egg pans to clean does make it easier still; and although it isn't much quicker than the conventional way of making them – there is a lot of opening and closing the microwave door to be done – it does make them bulk bigger, and this gives the dish a much more delicate feel. See p. 107 for a recipe.

Poached greengages

Cooking greengages conventionally and keeping them looking nice is an impossibility. The skins split and curl, the flesh disintegrates and the stones become detached; only if the cooking liquor is made impossibly sweet can this be prevented. With the micro it is possible to present whole green plums at table looking very pretty and also cooked inside. See p. 148.

Poppadoms

This crisp pancake, served with savoury dishes all over India, is traditionally grilled or fried, but now it can be microwaved. The microwaved flavour is not as peppery as a grilled one nor as bland as a fried one. Pile up three or four poppas (readily available in packets in oriental stores or supermarkets in all sorts of flavours) and micro until bubbled all over. When cool they will become crisp. Make sure that all of the poppa is bubbled, or at least not transparent, since raw poppa isn't pleasant in the mouth. For complete success, the poppas should be fresh, i.e. fairly flexible with no hard edges.

Preserving uses

Drying by microwave is an alternative way of preserving if your freezer is full.

Herbs

When you have a herb garden, it is easy to become blasé about the riches on your doorstep. Just to be able to dive into the greenery and emerge with a bouquet of four or five fresh, aromatic herbs is rapture to a creative cook. With herbs there is either a glut or a famine, so in summer, when there is so much about, it seems a bit daft to let it go to waste.

For the strongest aroma, harvest herbs just

before flowering time. The old fashioned method of laying them out in the sun to dry will do, but if there is a microwave handy the speed of micro-drying retains more of the essential aromatic oils. It also preserves some of the chlorophyll green so that they look better than sun-dried ones. Bright green herbs benefit most from this process.

Remove the stalks and lay the foliage, finger deep, in the oven between sheets of absorbent paper to soak up the steam. Allow the herbs to become crisp dry – just 4 minutes at full power will dry a couple of ounces. Keep them really dry in airtight jars, out of the light.

Mushrooms

A big haul of wild mushrooms is too special to be used all at once and they dry well in the micro. Cut up large specimens into attractive slices; small ones (with 1 in/2.5 cm caps or less) can be dried whole. Place in a single layer on double sheets of absorbent paper and cover with two more sheets. Micro for 3 minutes at full power. Turn the mushrooms over and micro again for 2 minutes more. Leave to dry out thoroughly in a warm dry place and keep them in an airtight jar.

Use them – after soaking them in boiling water for 15 minutes – to give a dish of mild cultivated mushrooms authority. See p. 126, garlicky mushrooms.

4 After Cooking

Flavour and Texture

It is tempting to think that once food has been cooked, it needs no further work and can be served forthwith. Maybe it can, but cooking reduces the individual flavours of ingredients to a common, cooked taste, and inevitably any fresh tastes (such as those found in vegetables, fruit and, most crucially, herbs) are lost. Happily these brilliant fresh topnotes can be restored to the dish with surprisingly little effort.

Brightness

It is really good practice to reserve a little of a bright-flavoured ingredient in the recipe so that it can be added, chopped fine, right at the last moment or two of the cooking. Fresh herbs benefit most from this treatment.

If these last-minute additions can't be seen, so much the better – they'll be more of a surprise. To see what effect this can have, try adding little bits of fresh Bramley apple to a smooth apple sauce or finely chopped onion to a meat gravy seconds before the cooking stops. Another way, with savoury dishes, is to serve brightness as a side dish in the form of a relish, like gremolata or pesto (see pp. 137–8).

Adjusting the taste

A dish should have a balance of stimulants for the tongue. Should the stimulus of saltiness or sweetness seem lacking, the usual way of putting that right is to add salt or sugar but, by adding a salty or sweet substance (olives or honey, for example), extra depth and novelty are to be had at the same time. Other stimulants and substitutes are suggested on pp. 80–92.

If the flavour of a savoury dish seems listless, and it can happen if the stimulants are evenly balanced, turn to chilli – it adds sparkle. I hasten to say that if your guests can taste it as hot, you've probably added too much. There is an earlier stage of chilli heat which is not hot but bright – you'll know what it is but your guests shouldn't be able to guess. Using raw chillies is hazardous: some are hotter than others even if they look the same and are out of the same batch – so it is easy to overdo it. Take away the guesswork by using chilli vinegar or oil, which can be added drop by drop (see p. 166). Don't restrict your thinking on chilli to savoury dishes, a little in custard is exquisite.

Pepper and mustard add heat in quite a different way – more tingling than bright – and more obviously too. Most people can recognize the taste of pepper, and that makes a dish less novel. However, mustard does have a bonus which should be taken advantage of: it accentuates the flavour of a sauce at the same time as adding heat.

Fresh horseradish is different again. Its heat is more ethereal and effects the nasal passage in a way that the others do not. For the best effect, with its tingle at its strongest, it must be used soon after it is grated. Don't even think about substituting with bottled horseradish.

Texture

Food with a crisp texture stands little chance of retaining it if left for any time in hot steamy dishes – which is a pity. Of all the textures, crispness is the most alive, the one most noticed by people when eating.

Water chestnuts and, to a certain extent, bamboo shoots do keep their crunch during cooking, but, these apart, giving crisp texture to a cooked dish is a matter of adding it when it can't be affected by humid conditions.

Fried nuts and croutons keep some of their crunch if they are not stirred into food but used as a topping at the last. They are alright in a salad, too, sprinkled on after the dressing has been folded in.

Black glutenous rice, dry not boiled, pops if fried in hot oil and keeps its crunch for quite a time when stirred into boiled rice.

Celery, carrots, radishes and apples also stay crisp for a short time in hot food – I often throw a spoonful of raw chopped carrot into a stew before serving for the extra taste and texture it gives.

Consistency of Sauces

Apart from adjusting the flavour and texture of a sauce, there is another factor that affects the enjoyment of eating. Dry food is unpleasant to eat; succulent food, by which I mean food with enough juice in or on it to make it easy to swallow, also allows its flavour to react with the taste buds better. This desirable state, the liquidity or juiciness of food, is often supplied by the sauce it comes with, and for maximum succulence it should be the thickness of thin cream, for the following reason.

A sauce gets into the mouth in two ways. Either it sticks to the solids which it is served with, or it can be spooned into the mouth with the solids, which is fine if the dish happens to be a sweet one and a spoon is to hand. But savoury dishes are eaten with a knife and fork, and so only the sauce that sticks to solid food will be enjoyed. Too thick a sauce isn't as succulent; too thin a sauce doesn't stick to the solids and is left behind on the plate. However, a sauce that has the consistency of thin cream not only sticks to the food but, once in the mouth, gives the right amount of succulence too. Or so it seems to me. No matter what explanation is the right one, thin cream is *the* most pleasing texture for a sauce to have.

Adjusting the thickness of sauces

Thinning down a thick sauce to the desirable, thin cream consistency presents few problems. It is all too simple to add more liquid, and the worst that can happen is a dilution of flavour. But there are several ways of thickening a thin sauce and it is a question of choosing the most appropriate one.

Reduction

This doesn't work with all sauces. Reducing

vegetable stock simply strengthens the flavour without changing its consistency, so for that use a purée thickener of the same ingredient (see below).

Reduction works well with savoury, protein-based stocks. If there is too much juice, strain out the solids, lest they get overcooked, and reduce the liquid by fast boiling – the wider the pan in which this is done, the faster the reduction. How far this reduction can be taken rather depends on the strength of the flavour already present, since that will become concentrated in the process. Always under-season before cooking, it's so much easier to add more than mask a surplus.

Reduction can be taken as far as a glaze: the point at which the sauce begins to change viscosity, the bubbles become smaller and any fat that may be around – provided there isn't too much of it – becomes emulsified into the body of the sauce, giving it a sheen. Meat fat has a lot of flavour and having it in a sauce really enriches its taste. Not all fats are beneficial however; some, like the fat from well-hung game or strong fish oil, are too rank to incorporate and should be skimmed off.

Getting rid of excess fat

Today the general consensus in the West is that fat floating on a sauce looks disgusting, desirable as it may be for flavour and mouth feeling. A little can be emulsified into the reduction, and it will stay that way for quite a while if it is kept warm and stirred occasionally. A splash of acidity – lemon juice or white wine – will help with this. Excess fat can be removed by freezing the sauce and scooping off the solidified fat. This removes all the fat and is the easiest way if you have the time. If not, move the sauce in its pan to the side of the heat and simmer. This drives the floating fat to the side furthest from the heat, where it can be scooped off without removing too much of the stock.

Sometimes a sauce will be too thin to hold the fat in emulsion. This calls for an agent to thicken it to the right consistency and hold the fat molecules in suspension.

Thickening agents

Flour

Wheat flour is the usual agent. It leaves a floury taste but that can be boiled out in time. For those who consider a floury taste undesirable, cornflour is a better bet. What little taste it has almost disappears with cooking, and the finish, look and texture of it are smoother. Best of all are arrowroot and potato flour. Both of these root flours thicken more than corn or ordinary wheat flour, and arrowroot has no perceptible taste at all. Of these four, wheat flour is the one which clouds the sauce most. But with fat in the sauce it will be slightly cloudy whatever you use.

A lumpy sauce is inevitable if dry flour is stirred into a hot liquid. Mix flour with enough cold liquid to make it the consistency of thin cream before stirring it into the sauce, off the boil, and lumps will not be a problem. As a rough guide to quantity, a teaspoon of flour, with enough liquid to make a thin cream, should emulsify $\frac{1}{4}$ pint/140 ml of liquid to the ideal sauce consistency. I say 'should', but it depends on the amount of fat present. Better to underestimate the thickening than overdo it – you can't take it out.

A faster but riskier way of adding wheat flour to a fatty stock is to take the sauce off the boil and sprinkle a little flour onto the floating fat (I keep a sugar caster loaded with flour by the stove, it distributes evenly). Wait for a few seconds – for the fat to absorb it – then stir the sauce and bring it back to the boil. Repeat the procedure if necessary.

Egg yolks

Use yolks instead of flour when richness is needed. They give a beautiful silky sheen to a sauce, which feels lovely in the mouth. But the liaison is delicate, and if the sauce is allowed to get anywhere near boiling, it will separate. A temperature over 60°C/140°F is enough to curdle the mixture. No matter how much blending is done to get back the liaison, the texture will never be as smooth again nor as creamy. I find the following way fairly foolproof.

Blend a yolk with twice its volume of sauce or other liquid. Add this to the hot sauce (a reasonably hot sauce means that you don't have to stir it so long) and heat and beat until it thickens. Do this slowly, don't leave the pan for a second, and the moment the sauce starts to thicken – the usual way to tell when that happens is when it begins to coat the back of the spoon doing the stirring – whisk it off the heat. It is prudent to stand the cooking pan in cold water for a minute or two at this stage as the sauce may continue to thicken, or even curdle, in the residual heat. As a guide, one small yolk will emulsify a $\frac{1}{4}$ pint/140 ml of liquid to sauce thickness. Yolks are particularly good with chicken and fish sauces.

Cream

Double cream doesn't thicken as well as flour or yolks, but it is superlative at producing a rich smoothness in the mouth and it makes the sauce look and taste creamy. Unfortunately cream masks flavour, but that won't matter if the sauce is gutsy and it can be an absolute lifesaver when a sauce has been over-seasoned.

Blending

Blend cooked, soft vegetables – carrots, parsnips, onions or celeriac, for instance – into a purée and use it as a good substitute for flour to thicken a sauce (a ready-made purée, like concentrated tomato purée, shouldn't be overlooked here). Using purée gives a grainy texture to sauce but the addition of cream helps make it smoother.

Other ingredients

There are some very effective and novel thickeners not normally considered for this role: ground almonds or walnuts, for instance, or toasted nut purées like hazelnut or peanut butter or coconut cream. These not only thicken but add a more positive flavour to a sauce. Unsweetened chocolate powder, the traditional thickener for *mole* sauce (see p. 123), makes it so rich that it needs cutting with chilli or lemon juice; a little is quite stunning in goulash.

Of course, if the sauce is to be served cold you can use gelatine, in the proportion of $\frac{1}{4}$ oz (7 g) to $\frac{1}{2}$ pint (285 ml) or agar agar, a tasteless extract of seaweed, if you have vegetarians at table.

Dealing with pan juices

Sometimes there aren't enough juices for a sauce. I'm thinking here of meat (roasted or cooked in a pan under a grill), roasted chicken or fried fish, when to have juices left in the pan usually means that the food has been over-cooked. To make sauces for these dishes, it is usual to deglaze the pan of its encrusted juices and fat by adding liquid – usually stock or wine, or both – and boiling them madly until any residue has been dissolved into the sauce. This boiling gets rid of any alcohol present. There was a time, in my salad days, when I thought that to waste all that alcohol was criminal, not realizing that alcohol has a strong effect on the palate and tends to blanket other flavours.

Unless a tasty, well-reduced stock is to hand (it always can be with frozen stock cubes, see pp. 162–3), even this liaison can be a bit thin and will need building up. Consider the use of packet stock cubes or MSG for flavour, or the addition of cream for texture.

Although wine is the usual vehicle for deglazing, it can be interesting to use other alcoholic liquids. Cider is splendid with pork, and beer (Guinness, for instance) makes a rich hoppy combination with gravy for roast beef and lamb.

Postscript

When trying to make a dish taste as you think it should and it is nowhere near what you had in mind, draw comfort from the fact that the good taste you aimed for is not the only one possible with the ingredients used. It is a little disappointing not getting the perfect taste bulls-eye – a good proportion of the food that goes out of my kitchen doesn't – but that doesn't interfere with others' enjoyment of it. Once or twice, when I was just beginning, I apologized for the taste not being how I intended – quite fatal. These days I never explain but give the food a fighting chance to speak for itself, and so should you.

5 Recipe Analysis

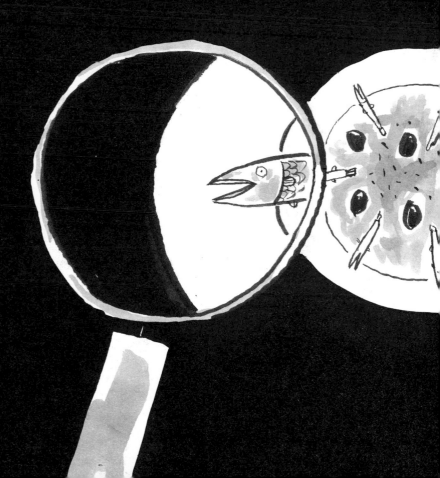

The usual way of looking at a recipe is to see it as a list of ingredients with instructions for assembly and treatment, whether with heat or not, so as to create a dish more delicious than the individual components. Provided all the ingredients are to hand, the recipe well written, the techniques familiar and care exercised in the preparation, the production of a decently edible dish is a betting certainty, and therein lies the attraction. Unfortunately, recipe instructions do not normally allow for human fallibility, and if anything should go wrong – there has been too heavy a hand with the salt or something has been a little burnt – it can be a major disaster. But there is often a way out of these situations if you understand how a recipe works and can, for instance, compensate for the over-use of one taste by adding another one, thereby restoring the recipe's original balance. However, even rescuing a dish can still mean you are tied to a recipe and to the ingredients it asks for. And being tied means more or less the same dish time after time, which gets boring.

At this stage you can of course master a new recipe, but looking at a familiar recipe in a different way can rejuvenate it so that, while it is still easy to prepare, the end result will be subtly different from the original. It will be adventurous to make, calling for imagination, and just as delicious to eat but in a new way. Rather than making sure you have the ingredients asked for, consider the stimulation each one gives to the palate and use whatever is to hand to provide the same stimulus.

If, for instance, a recipe calls for lemon juice, it could just as easily be replaced by citric acid powder. It wouldn't have a lemon smell, but if that were fundamental to the dish, then lemon zest would more than make good the deficit. But if the smell isn't important, further alternatives would be wine vinegar, rhubarb, sorrel or a sour Bramley apple. These contain different acids of course, and can be tasted as different, but they all supply the requirement for acid in a recipe, which needs it, say, to cut the cloying richness of a sauce.

Using different ingredients to provide the same taste stimulus does need some imagination – and not a little nerve – but there are some lists of possible substitutes at the end of the chapter to help with this.

The business of being creative with a recipe doesn't stop with substituting other ingredients to arrive at approximately the same taste. Trial and error will soon lead to completely different taste balances, enjoyably novel to both cook and eater. The golden rule when experimenting is never attempt to adjust the taste of the whole dish, always try it with a sample first.

Taste isn't the only factor in making a dish enjoyable, and the potential for stimulating other senses (such as those that register textures in the mouth, colour and temperature – for a full list see pp. 9–17) shouldn't be overlooked. After a little practice at reading a sound recipe and successfully playing with its tastes, it will soon be clear how these other senses have been catered for. Once that stage has been reached, you will be creating equally stimulating dishes of your own and be able to use a cookbook as an inspiration not a rule book.

Understanding Recipes

When reading a recipe for the first time, run through it first to get the feel of it; you may be able to compare its technique to one you have already mastered, which will make life a lot easier. Seek out the main stimulants in the list of ingredients and establish which of them you have. Substitute those you haven't with similar ones confident that the end result won't be a million miles away from the original in terms of stimulation and taste. Showing how this process works will best be served by an example or two. As in the cooking chapter, I'll give the bald recipe first just to give an idea of the sort of dish we're making.

I'm starting with an old favourite as most readers will know what good, or bad, bread and butter pudding tastes like and won't have to leap into the kitchen to find out what is being talked about – it's easier to imagine if the taste is in your mind already.

Bread and butter pudding

This dish is nostalgia alley to those who were reared on it. Really, it is nothing more than bread and milk de luxe, and the way it gets its 'luxe' is an object lesson in taste enrichment. Here, every part of the original 'bread soaked in warm sweetened milk' dish has been enhanced to appeal to an adult palate.

Serves 4
4–6 oz (115–170 g) sliced bread, usually white
1–2 oz (30–55 g) butter
1–1½ oz (30–45 g) sultanas (or other dried fruit)
15 fl oz (425 ml) milk (or milk and cream)
3 large eggs
4–5 oz (115–140 g) sugar
freshly ground spice to taste (like cinnamon, mace or nutmeg)

Butter the slices of bread (fresh or stale) and sprinkle generously with sultanas and lightly with freshly ground spice. Layer up the bread attractively in an ovenproof dish. Ideally, the bread should fill the dish so that the top will brown evenly later. Make a pattern with the top layer of crusts to increase eye appeal. Mix eggs, sugar and milk and soak the bread generously with it. Cook in a medium oven for around 30 minutes until the liaison has set to a custard. Sprinkle the patterned top with sugar and brown in the top of the oven or under the grill.

How the recipe works

Taste Sweetness is there, but honey or golden syrup would increase its depth. There is almost no salt apart from a little in the bread so be sure to use salted butter. A pinch of salt in the custard mix would be helpful. Sourness is pretty light – there is only the residual sharpness in the sultanas, fine for a youngster but not enough for an adult palate. Soak the sultanas in lemon juice before cooking or lace the surface with sweetened raspberry juice and then top with the sugar, before grilling. Bitterness is supplied by the bread crust but if you want more of it, toast the bread before buttering.

Smell A pleasant aroma will come from the spice and also when the surface is browned, but this can be heightened by flavouring the custard with vanilla or some lemon zest. Splashing alcohol onto each portion when serving helps too.

> If you use a vanilla pod to flavour the custard (simmer it in the milk for half an hour), it can be saved for another day by rinsing it clean of milk solids, drying it out and keeping it in a jar of sugar which will benefit from the company. Reuse it until exhausted then split the pod and use the seeds for one final custard.

Look The overall colours, cream and brown, are not particularly stimulating, and a contrast in red, orange or green might be helpful. A spot or two of raspberry purée, a dribble of concentrated orange juice or a sprinkle of chopped angelica, candied or fresh, would increase the visual excitement, and the sharpness of raspberries or orange juice would be excellent for lifting low acidity. But some would say that the cream and brown colours are homely, as is the pudding, and that the glossy brown of the caramelized sugar is quite enough, thank you. There is a part of me that agrees with that too, but here I'm suggesting different colours and flavours, which will allow the pudding to be different with every making.

Texture The feeling of soaked bread in the mouth, its spongy succulence, is enhanced by the buttery, all-round-the-mouth effect and the chewiness of the sultanas. This pudding doesn't have crunch, apart from a little in the crust. Toasted nuts, added at the last so that they don't lose their bite, would put this right. Split almonds (see p. 140) would be luxurious, but peanuts are quite satisfactory too.

The total effect of adding all these stimulants to the basic recipe might make it extremely rich, but there is no need to include them all.

Variations

The bread can be any colour: it is more important that the texture is firm enough to withstand total disintegration. Cake textured bread collapses into a porridge when soaked, depriving the dish of succulence. A nice variation uses brown bread, treacle, sultanas soaked in rum and powdered ginger as the spice. Using another filler instead of bread would give this dish a different name, but clearly rice pudding or macaroni pudding are in the same family, the main difference being that the filler – rice or pasta – is cooked in the sauce. The improvements suggested above will work equally well with these different fillers too.

Butter is pretty important, nothing enriches in quite the same way. A bland oil would be an inferior substitute but purified lard is tolerable. Lardy cake, for instance – an irresistible, fatty and sweetened sultana bread – is a very satisfactory replacement for white bread and sultanas and it brings its own enrichment in the shape of lard.

Sultanas can be replaced with currants or raisins (all are dried grapes) or almost any other dried fruit: chopped apricots spring to mind but prunes are good too. Fry them a little brown for even more taste. Soaking dried fruit in alcohol is a nice twist. Mincemeat, with its mix of dried fruit, candied peel and suet, would obviously fit the bill in more than fruit substitution – very Christmassy. A more summery pudding could use chopped, fresh, sweet fruit such as ripe bananas, pears, apples, stoned cherries or seedless grapes. Some people like to include jam as well as fruit.

Milk is essential, but it could be enriched with cream – which would be superior – canned milk (condensed or dried) or even a mild yoghurt or soured cream for a little extra sharpness.

Eggs as a thickening agent are the most suitable for this pudding, but they can overcook and separate. Custard powder, with its built-in thickener, could replace the egg and, mixed with milk, would be liquid enough to penetrate the bread before cooking.

All of these substitutions will not produce a traditional bread and butter pudding but will give equally satisfying variations on the theme.

Bramley mulligatawny soup

Sharp and salty soups are found everywhere, proof enough of their universal appeal. This version blossomed with a glut of apples in our orchard. Customers to the restaurant loved it and, since it is easy to make, it was an almost constant feature on the menu in the apple season.

Serves 4
1 lb (455 g) Bramley apples
1 pint (570 ml) chicken stock (or enough for a
*   thin cream consistency in the final soup)*
6 oz (170 g) onions
2 tablespoons garlic oil (see p. 165)
1 teaspoon ground coriander
½ teaspoon turmeric
½ teaspoon ground pepper
salt and chilli to taste
4 dessertspoons whipped cream, slightly salted
a pinch of toasted cumin seed

Dice the onions into small ¼ in (6 mm) pieces and fry them in a saucepan in garlic oil, coloured with turmeric and flavoured with ground coriander seed, pepper and chilli, until the onions are a little brown. Quarter the whole unskinned apples and cut them into ¾ in (2 cm) cubes; then put them into the pan with the onions and add the stock. Cook until the apple flesh has separated from the skin, then pass all through a mouli. Adjust for salt. Serve with a dollop of whipped cream and a sprinkled line of toasted cumin seed.

How the recipe works

Cooking all the apple produces more flavour – the core and seeds have a taste of their own. Well-flavoured chicken stock could just as easily be packet chicken cubes in this recipe – the gelatinous quality of good stock isn't essential here, although it would be nice. The fried onions and spices add a rich flavour core to the acid purée. A mouli extracts enough of the apple to thicken the soup but it could be pressed through a sieve if you haven't a mouli. The cream adds smoothness; it is put on at the last, partly as a colour contrast, partly to stop the acid in the soup from curdling it. Whipping keeps the cream afloat and looking pretty. The cumin seed not only enhances the spice content, it gives the teeth something to bite on; toasting accentuates the aroma of cumin and adds a little bitterness.

Variations

We used apples because they were there. Any sharp fruit will do as well – sour grapes, gooseberries, rhubarb or plums are all satisfactory but have less liquid than Bramley apples so more stock will be needed.

Curry powder can be exchanged for the spices but its known taste will be recognized. This won't spoil the balance of flavour but it will prevent any thinking about what spices have been used so the attention span will be shorter. On the other hand a spoonful of an Indian pickle – which is sour and hot and harder to identify as a flavouring – boiled with the apples will be more mysterious. Any Indian pickle will do but perhaps, considering the acidic nature of this soup, ginger or aubergine pickle will be better than lime. Steer clear of garlic pickle with its hint of stale garlic powder.

This soup was fathered by a curried parsnip soup (see p. 98), which was fashionable in the Sixties. Nowadays I make lentil and tamarind soup which is in the same flavour area and which has that pleasing, gum-sucking texture that cooked lentils bring to the mouth.

Substitute Stimulants

In the two recipes analysed above, many of the substitute stimulants occurred to me while searching for the culinary equivalent of the philosopher's stone – the magical, completely novel taste. There is no such animal of course, but I soon realized that, when dealing with the taste balance of a recipe, many different ingredients will trigger a reaction in the taste buds geared to respond to, say, sweetness and that it is reasonably safe to exchange one sweet ingredient in a recipe for another. Those who aren't used to questioning recipes will find the lists below useful as a start to working out their own lists of interchangeable stimulants.

These lists are far from comprehensive and only experience can tell which will be the most suitable for the particular stimulation required. Direct comparison of one with another in the experimental dish is the safest way of finding this out. Testing with minute amounts in a limited area of the dish enables any unwanted tastes to be stirred into the whole without ruining the final effect.

Salt

Salt comes in many forms, but sea salt seems the very essence of saltiness and at its most potent when added at table as small crystals and eaten before they have time to dissolve.

The other items in this group are compounded with salt. These compounds bring other tastes to a dish as well as saltiness and that is what makes them more exciting to use than salt alone. I've indicated where I find them useful when I can; proceed with caution.

Anchovies These small, salted fish have a flavour that enriches savoury dishes, with hardly a trace of fishiness. I use them in a tomato sauce for pasta and in goulash. Using fish and meat in combination is quite common: in Italy tuna goes with veal, in England oysters enrich a steak and kidney pie.

Seaweed The sort that comes from Japan in a sheet, Nori, has a salty taste (no surprise about that). Grill it to bring out its flavour and sprinkle over vegetables or beancurd as a novelty, or moisten it with soya sauce and wrap it around cylinders of rice. Do this when the rice is cooked and warm but unrinsed, so that it clings together and is easier to handle. Japanese rice tends to cling anyway.

Balachan This is rotted prawn or shrimp preserved in salt as a block. Its pungent flavour is to be used with caution. If you can taste it you have used too much, although the Indonesians, who use a lot of it, would hardly agree. I grate it into a fish soup or into a creamy prawn sauce for extra richness. A little in laksa doesn't go amiss. (See p. 96.)

Bombay duck This salted and dried fish comes from India. Fry it crisp, and crumble it over spicy Indian dishes – it is splendid with egg curry. Don't be put off by its smell when frying; open the windows instead – it is worth it. Those of a tender disposition who hate the smell of over-ripe Camembert had better forget about this.

Oyster sauce This is a compound of oysters decomposed in salt, which may sound disgusting but tastes delicious. I first met this sauce poured over a well-charred steak sprinkled with fresh grated horseradish. It is still my favourite combination with steak, although my preferred brand, Yu Kwen Yick, which actually tastes of the sea, if not of oysters, seems to have given way on the Chinese supermarket shelves to something much sweeter and less salty. The new brand is not as complementary but still alright.

Soy sauce Soy sauce is a must in the kitchen if you have an aversion to using MSG in its manufactured form, since it is present naturally in soya, its original source material. There are some terrible, inferior brands about; the best for me is Japanese – the light and bright Kikkoman – now widely available. Use soy when both salt and colour are needed.

Olives These are both salty and bitter, so using them can serve a double function. Now that they are to be found puréed and in jars, I use olives as a last-minute flavour adjustment more often. For delicious crostini spread it on toast, sprinkle with Parmesan and dried herbs and grill sharply.

Salt ham and bacon These come loaded with salt. I use them to deepen the flavour of soups and casseroles, but mostly the bacon is chopped fine, fried crisp and used in sauces. There is quite a jolt of salt from these condensed chewy pieces apart from the extra texture they give to a smooth sauce.

Sweet

Nothing is more naturally sweet than refined sugar. Molasses, extracted from sugar in the refining process, is not so sweet but has an almost fudgy richness making it an attractive variation to pure sugar. Experiment with molasses in chocolate confections and as the sweet content in vinaigrette and in savoury dishes. Caramelized sugar brings complex toffee overtones to recipes.

Fructose Available fairly generally in food supermarkets with other sugars, fructose is worth a special mention. It is the sweetener par excellence for fruit, turning sour fruit ripely sweet in a way not easy to detect. Using beet (or cane) sugar for the same purpose is alright, but when the two are compared, side by side, the sucrose in beet sugar really stands out. Fructose, which is twice as sweet as ordinary sugar, is a valuable aid when making fresh fruit dishes.

Honey Use honey where character as well as sweetness is needed.

Dried fruit There is a whole area of cooking that marries savoury dishes with the occasional sweet bite from a bit of sweet fruit, and because fruit has more concentrated sweetness when dried, it makes more of an impact.

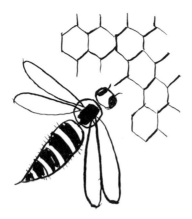

There are some classic fruit/savoury com
binations: pork with prunes, ham with pine-
apple, turkey and cranberries, savoury fried
rice with currants. A salad of fresh spinach
leaves with fried dried apricot slices and salted
toasted pine kernels tickles every taste bud on
the tongue.

Ripe fruit I do enjoy ripe fruit in a savoury
salad, and chopped fresh fruit is a splendid
corrective to an over-salted sauce.

Sour

Several acids register as sour in the mouth.
Each has a different flavour but not to the
acid-detecting taste buds where the overriding
effect is the same. A combination of two or
three gives a tremendous aurora of acidity. The
list gives derivatives so that you can try this
out for yourself.

Citric acid All citrus fruit have this acid,
lemons and limes most obviously, but Seville
oranges are almost bitter sharp and should be
considered for more than marmalade. Citric
acid is available as a refined powder sometimes
referred to as lemon powder for obvious
reasons. I keep some on the shelf as a last resort
if a lot of acid is needed, in a stew for instance,
and there are no lemons to hand.

If acid is not needed for adjustment purposes
but the presence of citrus would be good, use
zest alone. I like the clean tingle it gives to
fried rice. Use a morsel of fresh orange zest to
turn Darjeeling tea into a very superior Orange
Pekoe. No zest should be thrown away; I use
more lemon zest than juice in the kitchen.

Malic acid All apples have this acid, but
dessert apples have sugar as well, which may
not be needed. Unripe green apples and the
wonderful Bramley cooking apple are nicely
acidic with little sweetness, so they are the
ones to be considered here. Use them to bright-
en and lighten mincemeat or, diced small, with
elderflowers in May-time pancakes or in rich
pork gravy.

Tartaric acid This acid, together with malic
and citric, gives wine its sharpness, but it is
allowed to develop more strongly in wine
vinegar. A refined and much stronger version

is available as cream of tartar powder, but it has a twang without the malic and citric acids to temper it – use it as a last resort. Traditionally it gives sharpness to fruit jams, home-made lemonade and toffee. It is combined with baking soda to make the powerful raising agent known as baking powder.

Oxalic acid This is the acid that makes rhubarb and spinach sour and sorrel even more so. Sorrel has so much acid that when it is cooked, and the acid released, it turns from chlorophyll green to a sludgy green-brown. Unfortunately there is no way of avoiding this, so I tend not

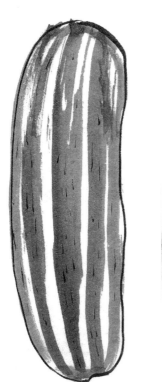

to make sorrel soup (unless I cheat by adding spinach), and stick to using it raw in salads. I grow a pretty, small, spade-shaped leaf variety called Buckler's Sorrel for that. Use diced pink rhubarb in fruit cake, in duck gravy instead of the more usual black cherries or orange and as a kick to overcooked spinach which has lost its acid (it looks good there too).

Lactic acid Milk turns sour because of this acid, but it is more handy to the cook in the stronger yoghurt form, at least for acidic purposes. It gives the delicious bite to the old Cheddar cheese that I prefer to use in stewed cheese (see p. 105).

Pickle and chutneys These should be considered when more than acid is needed. Chopped pickles are handy and unusual, mixed into stir-fried vegetables for instance. I have a passion for pickled capers, left whole in a sauce either for meat or fish. They are good in aubergine purée too.

Bitter

This is not the most obvious taste to be thought of as an improvement to the flavour of a dish, but a quick look at the list below will show how many desirable foods there are that have a distinct bitter quality. Since there are taste receptors that get a stimulus from bitterness, they may as well be catered for. It would be stupid to ignore their potential for focusing attention on a dish.

Burning food provides bitterness and is the easiest way of getting it (all too easy, some would say – getting rid of it is the problem). The process of burning starts with browning and that is not thought of as bitter or unpleasant, so it is a question of degree really. Popping a dish under a grill for a last-minute browning or, better yet, singeing it with a salamander (see p. 35) are good ways of getting the right amount of bitterness. Excess bitterness can be balanced out with sourness, which is useful to remember if you've had a disaster and burnt the food unintentionally.

Other forms of bitterness can also be used: very strong tea, instant coffee powder or unsweetened chocolate powder are unusual but effective in savoury dishes. I use chocolate powder as a partner to chilli in a Mexican dish called chicken *mole* (see p. 123).

Bitter herbs like sage, thyme and rosemary work to a degree, especially when burnt on a barbecue or under a grill, but bring lots of other flavours with them. Still if only a flick of bitter is needed, that might be enough.

Another unlikely agent is mustard whose bitterness can be used as a taste enhancer in moderation. Olives are bitter too and they are available as a purée in a jar – very handy.

Spice seeds – cardamom, cumin, mustard, caraway etc – are bitter, but they are mostly aromatic so they can't be used to add bitterness in any quantity. Most of them are improved by a little toasting which increases their bitterness as well as their aroma.

Other, more bizarre, carriers of bitter flavour include the skins of nuts, which are simply left on for bitterness; the juice of aubergines and courgettes – the reason for salting slices of these is to get rid of the bitterness (I quite like it left in, myself); and cucumber skin, which is bitter *and* indigestible – not so good. Citrus fruit albumen – the white part of peel – gives the bitter bite to marmalade and to lemon chutney (see p. 138).

As for Angostura Bitters, that well-known additive that turns gin pink, it *is* bitter in a medicinal, quinine, sort of way and rather nice in custard (giving it a little mystery) in place of the more usual vanilla or lemon zest.

Herbs

There are two main families – the Umbelliferae and the Labiatae – which dominate the herb world and substituting one for another within the same family will be a pretty safe thing to do. On the other hand, changing fresh herbs for dried is risky. Quarter the amount if dried herbs are used and remember that they take longer, much longer, to release their full potential. If fresh herbs are bought rather than gathered, it is a bit of a waste to use them early in the cooking process since their aromatic freshness is quickly lost with heating and they lose their lovely green colour at the same time. So, when fresh herbs are expensive or rare, substitute with dried herbs early on in the cooking process and keep the fresh herbs for last-minute addition.

The Umbelliferae family

These herbs, as the name implies, have seed heads that look like an upturned umbrella. The green foliage is considered a herb, but where the seeds are used in cooking, I deal with them under spices. (See coriander for an unusual halfway use.) Usually the edible, 'sweet' varieties have an anise flavour with parsley, celery and coriander flavours as the more obvious variants.

Anise flavours

Fennel This has the strongest anise taste of the better-known herbs and is found in two forms. The wild variety has the strongest flavour; I use the youngest, pale green fronds and the unopened flower heads in salads and the dark fronds in boiling water when cooking vegetables, as a change from using mint. The dried stalks make a distinctive smoke in a barbecue, fashionable when smoking fish. The other form is grown as a vegetable, with a bulbous white root tasting sweetly of anise. This is good in a salad with red peppers and walnuts or lightly parboiled (in a microwave preferably) and fried in browned butter.

Sweet cicely This is a large (3–4 in/7.5–10 cm) pretty, anise-flavoured plant. Stalk, leaf and root are all used, and all have a sweetness similar to dilute saccharin. One fanciful cook has even suggested it as an adequate sweetener for sour fruit like rhubarb. The amount needed to sweeten makes the rhubarb very anise indeed, but a morsel gives an interesting, indefinable twist to both rhubarb or apple purée. It is superb in salads, especially the pretty, clean-tasting, young flower heads. If it likes its growing site, it will become a perennial with its tender root thick enough to be considered a vegetable.

Chervil Chervil tastes like a milder version of sweet cicely. Lightly anise-flavoured parsley is as near as I can get to a description. It is pretty as decoration on plate or in salad. This is one of a group of herbs that the French specify under the title *fines herbes*. The others are chives, tarragon and parsley, and together they make a singularly aromatic and very 'French' taste.

Dill This is a sweet, light anise-flavoured, delicately fronded herb. Use the fronds in salad and the stalks in pickles and court-bouillon. Dried, it loses all its considerable ethereal charm. It is the smell of spring in this cook's garden.

Angelica Angelica stems are candied for use in cakes, just like candied peel. The flavour is also of anise but with a fabulous eau-de-Cologne top note, which makes it particularly suitable for use with sweet dishes — in fact the only Umbelliferae that works better with sweet than with savoury dishes. It makes a great surprise element in savoury or sweet salads. I love it with apple purée.

Parsley There are two sorts: curly leafed (the young, shorter stemmed stalks are more fragrant) and Hamburg or turnip-rooted, which is a coarser-flavoured and slightly more bitter variety. It has a flat leaf easily confused with coriander. The young, bright green leaves are sweet and are my favourite parsley taste.

Celery flavours

Celery Apart from the usual blanched celery on sale as a vegetable, there is a variety which is used as a herb. This has the look of a young, green, unblanched celery, with a much stronger celery taste than the sweeter blanched variety. It can often be found in Chinese supermarkets. Powerful and similar to lovage but not as aromatic.

Lovage This has, in my opinion, the best-flavoured and most aromatic of the celery tastes. Grow it in your garden or window box since it is rarely on sale. Use both leaf and stalk in food. The thin stalks, used sparingly, are quite stunning as part of a vegetable stir-fry, astringent and aromatic in a sweet way.

Celeriac Celeriac leaves can be used as a winter substitute for lovage but are bitter. Still they are better than nothing.

Coriander Coriander leaves, stalks and, as I discovered lately, roots can all be used. This plant has an unusual, almost soapy, perfumed taste (my herbal calls it fetid) – quite different to the dried, slightly orangy flavoured seed. This fragrance is quickly lost in the cooking process so keep a little to add at the last minute. All fresh herbs suffer the same way when cooked or dried. But a lovely Indian lady I know uses fresh coriander in prodigious amounts with her ginger chilli chicken. The aroma gets cooked out in the stew, as one would expect, and it tastes, after an hour's simmering, rather like a flowery spinach. This is simply wonderful combined with fresh, lightly cooked, ginger. By prodigious, I mean half a pound (225 g) per chicken.

Some years ago, I discovered that the green seeds of coriander have a very powerful, distinct flavour of their own – half way between the green leaf taste and the orange of the dried seed. These seeds are magic to cut a rich-flavoured rice. Preserve them in olive oil in the fridge and use the oil, sparingly, in a salad for a mysterious, sense-provoking top note.

The Labiatae family

This family has a wider taste variation than the Umbelliferae, ranging from a bright clean minty taste to an almost smoky aromatic wintergreen flavour. Some care has to be exercised when substituting one end of the flavour range with the other, mostly in the amounts used. The wintergreen flavours suffer the least of all in the drying process which is ironic since most are available fresh throughout the year in temperate climes.

Mint flavours

All the following are interchangeable but basil does have a particular affinity with tomatoes.

Mint There are two main varieties: peppermint, which provides the flavour most used in mint-flavoured sweets and toothpastes, and spearmint, which provides the flavour most used in mint sauce and again in toothpaste. The many other varieties include apple mint, eau-de-Cologne mint and ginger mint, all of which have a mint flavour but with a hint, in each, of the name they have been given. Apple mint seems the sweetest and is my favourite.

Basil I have working knowledge of three of the many varieties. Two of these I use with pleasure when I can get them: the small-leafed bush basil (which is fairly tolerant to regular pruning and the one most likely to succeed in a pot on an English summer window) and the red-leafed Far Eastern variety called Dark Opal. However, neither quite catch the full blown scent of the more commonly known, broad-leafed variety, sweet basil, which needs strong outdoor sunlight to develop its full aroma. Its scent is like a kind of savoury mint crossed with the smell of a newly picked ripe tomato. Nothing recalls more strongly the heat of summer sun on my back than this wonderfully aromatic favourite.

Smoky aromatic flavours

Most of the smoky aromatic herbs smell very alike to me and seem eminently interchangeable.

Thyme There are several forms, all tasting much the same except the lemon variety, which is zesty and very useful in ringing a change in a herby menu. The freshly opened flowers of thyme work a very nice visual trick with hot garlicky mushrooms (see p. 126).

Sage There is a useful purple variety, which is intriguing in a salad, for a moment at least. And there is dittany, a very pungent south Mediterranean herb, which looks like sage and shouts 'Greek' to me. It is very potently sage-

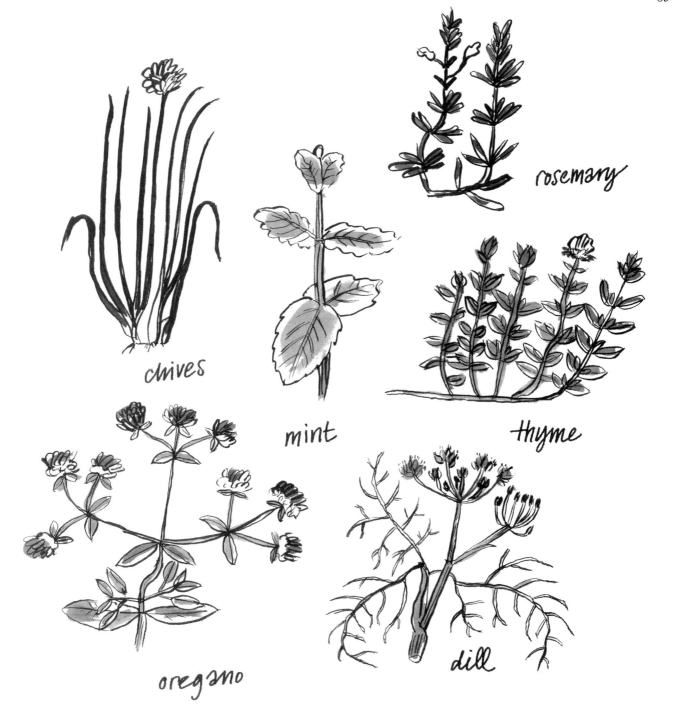

chives

mint

rosemary

thyme

oregano

dill

tasting and keeps its character a long time. I always bring some back with me.

Savory There are two sorts: winter, which is a perennial and wintergreeny, and summer – which isn't and is also less smoky than thyme. Summer savory is quite a bright herb and a favourite of mine, but it's a bit of a bother to grow, as it doesn't seem to be self-setting and needs freshly planting every year.

Rosemary Rosemary tastes like wintergreen and smells a bit medicinal. Although perennial, it is vulnerable to frost through open wounds if culled in winter. This is the only herb that seems as good dried as fresh, which is just as well given the above stricture. The prunings are used to flavour smoke in a barbecue or a smoking house.

Marjoram This is a cultivated, less pungent form of the wild oregano. Although this herb is often specified for use on pizzas and on many other dishes, I find that thyme and sage work equally well, especially if they get burnt, as they do on pizza.

Other families

There are a few herbs from other families that I use regularly.

Tarragon There are two varieties: Russian tarragon, which grows vigorously, rather like a tall weed, and has a bitter, slightly anise taste.

This shouldn't be confused with, or grown in place of, the sweeter, smaller, more aromatic and temperamental French tarragon, the fresh flavour of which lies between anise and fresh young meadow grass. It dries without losing too much of its aroma. The classic uses of tarragon are with chicken (see p. 40) and with béarnaise sauce, which is hollandaise sauce made green with tarragon.

French tarragon

Fenugreek Young plants of fenugreek look like corn salad and are used for much the same purpose. However, when its leaves are dried, they develop a strong smoky/sweet compost flavour. Crumble one of these into a stew and the smell of it stays on your fingertips all day. The seed is not so strong flavoured but is much loved by Indian cooks who seem blind to its all-enveloping pungency. This is the pre-dominant flavour in cheap curry pastes and pickles.

Spices

There is one family of spices, the ginger family, that deserves a special mention as it produces a variety of flavours that seem unconnected in their dried state but have an affinity when fresh. All members of this family are inter-changeable to a surprising degree and they are formidable in combination.

The ginger family

Ginger The part of the plant that has the flavour is the succulent root, or rhizome. Fresh, it has a brilliance and sharpness unimaginable to those who only know the dried root or ginger powder. It loses this aromatic top note when cooked, so save some fresh root to add just before serving.

Galingale This looks a bit like ginger and tastes similar but without as much fragrance and with more bitterness. As a dried powder called laos, galingale is much used in Indone-sian food. I met it first in a garlic and peanut sauce served with satay.

Turmeric Turmeric is usually found in the West as a yellow ochre powder. In this state you'd never guess it belonged to the ginger family, but fresh, the small orange-fleshed rhizome has a bright aroma similar to ginger. This juicy root can be found increasingly in oriental food stores and supermarkets. Use it grated fresh into hot cooked rice where its yellow juice

bleeds, colouring the rice immediately around it. The result is three-colour rice: orange from the turmeric flesh, yellow from the juice and white rice with an intriguing gingery top note. Don't stir a lot or all the rice will turn yellow.

Cardamom In this member of the family it is the seed heads that are used rather than the rhizome, but even so the flavour is still of the ginger family – I associate it with eau-de-Cologne somehow. One of my ambitions is to go to the Cardamom Hills in southern India and eat them from the plant. The little three-sided pods can usually be found in three forms, the unprocessed pale green, the puffy white and the larger more medicinal black pod. The green ones are most easily found and are, I think, marginally more aromatic. Be careful when buying and using these pods: only those with the shiny fresh black seeds have the true carda-mom flavour. Later they become dessicated, orange-coloured and taste stale. The new crop arrives in Europe about November, and what a difference in the flavour there is then.

Other families

The rest of the spices have pretty individual flavours. I'm not aware of any particular problem when substituting one for another except where personal association may strike the odd note, like using juniper with fruit when my association with it is with game. Spices seem to be either sweet or peppery. All have distinctive top notes of aroma, some more brilliant than others but interchangeable as far as the palate is concerned.

Nutmeg and mace Mace is the more aromatic and more digestible covering of nutmeg. I can only guess why cooks turn to the nut when the covering is so much better. It may be because the nut is always used, freshly grated, as required, and the mace is ground in quantity well in advance and loses its aroma in storage. Buy whole blades of mace and grind what you need freshly, wherever nutmeg is asked for.

Allspice The name says it all; it is similar in flavour to a combination of pepper, nutmeg, mace and cloves. Grind this spice as you need it, as its aroma is fugitive.

Cloves I have been sickened by an overdose of this spice in the past and it is difficult to overcome the association. It is useful to add depth and ring the changes in spice combinations (see p. 168), and I quite like it with caraway and cumin in a paprika; but on its own – not for me.

Cinnamon and cassia Cassia is a coarser variant of cinnamon with less sweetness and many more aromatic overtones. The conventional wisdom is to use cinnamon (which looks like a cigar) for sweet dishes and cassia (which looks like small pieces of bark) for savoury. I use cassia for both because I adore its aroma, and I grind my own as required.

Mustard, horseradish and radishes These are in the same flavour family. Horseradish has the best top note but it is fugitive and must be used fresh. Radishes are much milder, and their pickled seed pods are an alternative to capers.

Peppercorns These come black, white and green. Green are immature black peppercorns and are lighter and brighter-tasting than black; white are black peppercorns with their aromatic cases removed and are only used if pepperiness is needed in a white sauce where black peppercorn pieces would look unsightly.

Pink peppercorns These are bought pickled, in a jar. They look very pretty whole in sauces but are not really peppercorns even though they almost taste as if they were. They are said to be poisonous in large quantities.

Caraway and cumin These look-a-likes are herb seeds really. They are at their most stimulating when toasted. Toast them under the grill just before guests arrive so that their wonderful smell is hanging about as an appetizer. Other herb seeds, like fennel and coriander, also benefit from toasting.

6 Recipes

Stocks

So good has the quality of packeted stock cubes become that the use of the phrase 'well-flavoured stock' in recipes these days is almost always a euphemism for a stock cube and water. So why bother to go through the process of making your own? What a stock cube can't give you is the lip-smacking, all-round-the-mouth satisfaction that real home-made stock gives to a dish. Compare one directly with another and you will notice the difference

straight away. So make a habit of simmering old carcasses or joint bones in water and wine with pot herbs (by which I mean carrots, celery stalks, onions or leeks) and herbs. When strained, the resulting liquid is not in a very convenient form for the modern kitchen – it tends to be thinly flavoured and doesn't keep for long, even in a fridge. Make it more tractable by reducing it, by boiling, to a third of its former bulk, at which point it should set like a loose jelly (the comparison is apt, gelatine is the setting agent in both). It keeps for much longer then, and its flavour is more intense. At this stage, I freeze it into cubes and keep it in my deep freeze.

Fish stock

Fishmongers are usually glad to get rid of fish offal so always ask for some extra bones and skin when you buy fish. Insist on white fish bones; others, like mackerel, herring, rockfish and skate bones, add a curious, almost unpleasant taste to the stock.

2–3 lb (910–1400 g) white fish bones and skin
3 pints (1.7 litres) water
1 pint (570 ml) dry white wine or dry cider
3 sticks of celery
2 leeks
½ head (whole bulb) of garlic
3 medium-sized carrots
a handful of parsley or chervil (or other anise-
  flavoured herb)
5 bay leaves
5 juniper berries, crushed
1 level dessertspoon each of salt and peppercorns
1 teaspoon of sugar
zest of ½ lemon

Boil all together for half an hour (skimming off the scum if you need it clear for aspic), and then strain off the solids. Reduce, by boiling, to at least half its original volume, skimming still, then taste. If the stock is bitter, it could be that you have had fish heads in the stock. These are fine but only if the bitter gills have been removed first.

If it has a good lip-smacking fishy taste, you can add salt at this stage; if not, reduce it further. Cool and place in a basin in a fridge to set. Cut off the skin formed on the top, turn the jelly out of the dish and cut off any residue from the bottom. What is left should be transparent jelly – fish aspic in fact. Reduce it so that it sets to a stiff jelly if you are making frozen stock cubes from it.

Chicken stock

Use carcass bones left from a roast, add pot herbs (as in the fish stock recipe above) and simmer until the gristle holding the bones together has dissolved into the stock. For a fragrant stock, replace the pot herbs with a fresh supply half way through the simmer, adding some zest of lemon. Boil for 2 or 3 hours. Reduce to a glaze (see p. 72), leaving the salt adjustment until after the reduction.

Browned chicken stock

A different flavour can be had by roasting the bones until brown before starting the simmer. The taste is richer, but less obviously chicken and the colour is that of weak tea. This is just what the doctor ordered if you are planning a cold chicken in aspic (see p. 115).

Brown meat stock

The process is the same as for the browned chicken stock above. Extra richness can be had by browning the vegetables as well. I usually add a little lemon juice to the glaze before freezing.

Clarifying for aspic

For a transparent stock, lightly beat an egg white (1 egg white for each pint/570 ml of stock) into the melted stock and heat slowly, stirring hardly at all until nearly boiling. Strain through a sieve lined with a cloth. Reinforce with gelatine if it hasn't jelled enough for aspic.

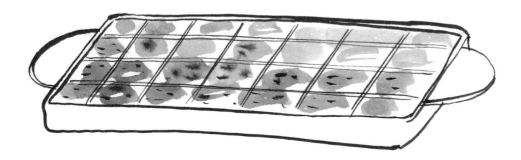

Soups

Lightning home-made vegetable soup

This soup was born in a moment of hunger desperation with kids crying and grown-ups awash with good beer but little else. The idea was to get a decent, substantial soup ready in double quick time.

Allow 7 fl oz (200 ml) of stock per person. I use any meat or poultry stock to hand or, failing that, water and stock cubes. This is put onto boil while a variety of vegetables are cleaned and cut up into pieces (suitably sized to fit easily onto a soup spoon). Those which take longest to cook are prepared first and put into the stock as soon as they are finished. So the order in the queue of ingredients might start with split lentils and dried herbs followed by root vegetables, then onions followed by other vegetables in order of softness, and finishing with tomatoes and fresh herbs. The cube or piece size varies: the first of two vegetables with similar cooking times being cut in larger pieces than those cut up second – on the reasonable assumption that the smaller the piece size, the faster the cooking time. The flow of ingredients into the soup stops when there seems to be as much solid matter as there is fluid.

And what should go into this concoction to make it memorable? I like lentils or pulses of some sort. Split lentils will cook within the fifteen minutes I usually set myself as a tolerable time for people to wait without protesting. Failing them, perhaps there is something suitable on the shelf like canned baked beans, peas or chickpeas. But rice or pasta can be used as the filling element, provided they are put into the stock fairly early.

Root vegetables and potatoes are obvious candidates and onions, or others of the same family (leek, spring onion, garlic or shallot) are essential. Celery (or celeriac, parsley or fennel) introduces a pleasantly clean taste. Apart from these, pretty well anything, in the herb or vegetable line, goes. I like tomatoes to be present in some form, fresh, canned or a purée, for the colour balance, if for no other reason. Fresh chilli gives authority if everyone likes it, and a squeeze of lemon adds depth at the last (you could use a slice or two of whole lemon cut up small, in which case start with that). Grated cheese – Parmesan for preference – will give a weak-flavoured soup a final enrichment. Pesto (see p. 137) is excellent as a pass-round-the-table relish.

Laksa

This Malaysian/Chinese fish soup has considerable presence and makes a substantial starter or a lighter main course. The soup base is made from well-flavoured fish or chicken stock, whitened with coconut cream, spiked with lemon grass and seasoned to taste. To this promising beginning is added slices of raw skinned chicken, raw fish balls, water chestnuts, shreds of fresh ginger and coarse-chopped spring onions. And finally, in goes a good handful of bean sprouts, chopped green coriander and some rice noodles. It is served with a pass-around bowl of oily red prawn sambal.

Serves 4 as a main course, 6 or 7 as a starter

Soup base
2 pints (1.1 litres) of good fish or chicken stock
2 heaped tablespoons coconut cream
zest of $\frac{1}{4}$ small lemon or lime, shredded – or 2 in (5 cm) lemon grass cut from the thick ends of two sticks in $\frac{1}{4}$ in (6 mm) slices

Garnishes
10 oz (285 g) chicken breast, sliced thin across the grain
10 oz (285 g) white boneless fish, made into raw fish balls
4 water chestnuts
4 large spring onions
1 in (2.5 cm) young ginger root, cut into match-sticks
3 oz (85 g) rice noodles, cooked soft
1 large handful bean sprouts
1 heaped tablespoon fresh coriander, coarsely chopped

Simmer the soup base ingredients for 10 minutes then add the chicken (in slices small enough to get onto a soup spoon) and fish balls.

Fish balls are made by blending the raw fish in a food processor (not so much that it becomes a purée – leave a little texture), then season with salt, pepper and a pinch or two of four-spice powder (see p. 167). Fashion the mixture into small, grape-sized balls and roll in flour. These fishballs can be prepared ahead and frozen without hurt.

After a couple of minutes add the water chestnuts. These should be washed, peeled and cut into small slices (canned chestnuts are around, but fresh are best: select the hard ones with no sign of softening around the neck or base).

Then add the noodles, fresh ginger, bean sprouts and spring onions. Return the soup to the boil, then add the coriander just before serving. To a plate of this white soup, with flecks of green, is added the visual excitement of a spoonful of brilliant ruby red prawn sambal (see p. 134).

It is fun to eat this soup the Eastern way, with chopsticks, drinking the liquid directly from the bowl that it is served in. Indulge in much slurping for maximum enjoyment. For more detail on laksa, especially planning ahead, see the menu on pp. 151–3.

Variations

The stock can be made of packet chicken or fish stock cubes – lobster soup cubes are rather nice. Add a little gelatine (about 1 teaspoon of powder for this quantity of soup) for an all-round-the-mouth taste.

Pork balls, made of fine-minced pork (seasoned with salt, pepper and ground mace), can replace the fish balls but the stock should be chicken or meat in that case.

Naval marrowfat pea soup (1940s style)

Serves 4
½ lb (225 g) dried marrowfat peas
1 teaspoon bicarbonate of soda
a ham bone or bits of ham and bacon rind
¾ lb (340 g) potatoes, peeled and cubed
seasoning to taste (experiment with sage, pepper,
 sugar and vinegar)

Cover the dried peas with twice the depth of water, stir in the soda until it is dissolved and leave overnight.

Drain the peas and rinse them, add the other ingredients and cover with enough water to give 1–2 in (2.5–5 cm) clear over the ingredients. Boil until soft, about 1½ hours. Pass through a sieve and adjust for salt (if there is too much, and there might well be with the ham bone in it, try to ameliorate with a little sugar or vinegar) and pepper.

This is how it used to be made in the Royal Navy, and it is still good out at sea, but for more usual, less ravenous, occasions I would have to adapt it somewhat – it would be death at the start of a four course meal.

Variations

Marrowfat peas are out because of the necessary addition of bicarbonate of soda and the flavour it brings with it; in would be lentils of any sort, split peas or dried beans. Potatoes are still a good idea as is some sort of ham, either a bone or, if you can get them, bacon rinds chopped up small to be simmered with the lentils. Good, too, is some enriching agent like butter or oil, which can be used to fry brown the onions, leeks or garlic that this recipe cries out for. The water should be a stock, but a stock cube is alright. Some fresh herb, added at the last, or some dried ones at the start are a good idea: mint would complement the ham nicely (even bottled mint sauce wouldn't be bad).

Cream of parsnip soup

Put simply, this is a well-flavoured stock in which chopped parsnips have been cooked until tender, and then the whole lot is puréed into a creamy but rather grainy soup and seasoned to taste. It needs a lot of help to qualify for a place in this book since each mouthful of it tastes the same, the colour is bland and its sweetness is a bit off-putting, not to mention the grainy texture. In the Sixties, when this soup was popular, cooks added curry powder

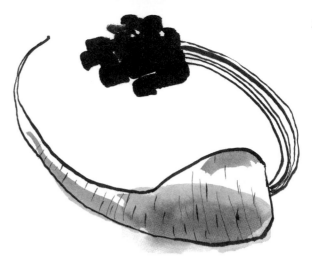

to cut the sweetness, but curry powder has a strong identity which eaters recognize, and so something else, not so obvious, is needed for a touch of mystery. I use tamarind and lemon zest here and, for a touch of spiciness, a sprinkle of toasted cumin as part of the decoration.

Serves 4
1½ pints (850 ml) chicken stock
½ lb (225 g) parsnips, peeled and chopped
4 oz (115 g) onion, chopped
4 oz (115 g) potato, chopped
1 oz (30 g) butter
1 oz (30 g) garlic oil
1 oz (30 g) fresh coriander stalks, chopped
1 tablespoon tamarind purée (whipping cream thickness)
salt and pepper to taste
2 teaspoons toasted cumin
a grate or two of lemon zest

First, a word or two on tamarind. To my knowledge it is available in two forms: dried and compressed in a block (with or without seeds) and as a purée, ready to go, in a jar. The dried sort needs to be soaked in hot water for upwards of an half hour and the resultant slurry passed through a mouli to get a thick purée; if it contains seeds, these will have to be removed first. Tamarind purée from a jar is very handy but, as is usual with this sort of convenience, there is a price to pay: the flavour, sharp though it is, lacks a fruity palm-date taste, but it is not needed for this soup, so reach for the tamarind jar not the mouli.

Brown the onions in the butter and garlic oil, add stock, potato and parsnip. Simmer until the parsnips are soft, purée the soup and add enough tamarind to make it sharp and bright – taste as you add, you may not care for a whole tablespoonful. Stir in the coriander stalks and lemon zest and reheat momentarily.

Serve with a swirl of lightly whipped cream floated onto each plate, over which sprinkle a line of toasted cumin crossed with a line of paprika. Toast the cumin just before the guests arrive, the smell is a wonderful appetite sharpener.

Variations

Substitute 7 oz (200 g) of lentils (any colour, split or whole) for the parsnips and add a stalk or two of celery or a good sprig of lovage, to make lentil soup with tamarind.

Substitute a thin Bramley apple purée for the parsnips and spike the soup with mango pickle to make a Bramley mulligatawny soup (see p. 79).

Goulashsuppe

This is a rich mahogany-coloured soup with
small bits of meat (and vegetables with a bit
of bite left in them), brightened with a dollop
of really sharp sour cream. Make fresh garlic
and green chilli relish (see below) to pass
around for colour and table interest.

Serves 4
1½ pints (850 ml) meat stock
*1 lb (450 g) minced lean beef or lamb, or even
    pork*
1 lb (450 g) onions, chopped
¾ lb (340 g) potatoes, diced
½ lb (225 g) carrots, diced
2 tablespoons celery, chopped
1 heaped teaspoon dried sage or mixed herb
4 bay leaves
2–3 juniper berries
½ oz (15 g) paprika
*salt to taste or ½ tin filleted anchovies or ½ teaspoon
    balachan*
2 tablespoons garlic oil
1 head (or whole bulb) of garlic, peeled
vinegar to taste

Relish
½ fresh chilli
1 clove garlic
salty vinegar to cover
2 tablespoons coriander, chopped
2 tablespoons green capsicum, chopped

Fry the onions, garlic, carrots and meat in the
garlic oil until they start to brown, then add
the paprika and the balachan or anchovies if
you're using them. Add stock, potatoes and all
the herbs and spices.

Simmer for an hour or so; remove the bay
leaves and the juniper berries if you can find
them, but don't worry if you can't. Taste the
soup and, unless it is already too hot, fry 2
teaspoons paprika in garlic oil and add this to
the soup. Taste for salt and sharpness – try a
drop of vinegar to one side of the pan to see if
that improves the flavour and add more if it
seems a good idea. Add celery and serve with a
bowl of soured cream and a green relish on the
table.

To make the relish, put some fine-diced chilli
and garlic into a salty vinegar with a pinch of
sugar. Let it marinate for 15 minutes, strain
and add plenty of fine-chopped coriander and
green peppers. You can use the strained vinegar
for the soup adjustment.

I've blithely assumed that you will be using
sweet paprika for this soup but if all you have
is the hot piquant sort go easy on the chilli in
the relish. The herby, lemony gremolata (see
p. 138) is good with this soup too.

Gazpacho

This simple cold Spanish soup is usually made with tomatoes but I like this green variation.

Serves 4
½ cucumber, peeled
3 oz (85 g) crustless white bread
4 tablespoons vinaigrette (see p. 132)
1 tablespoon parsley, chopped
1 green pepper, chopped
1 tablespoon garlic oil, browned
*1 tablespoon sweet Spanish onion or spring
  onion, finely chopped*

Blend all the ingredients, except the onion, with enough water to make this easy in a blender; then add enough chilled water to make a slurpy soup. Add the freshly chopped, sweet or spring onion just before serving.

Serve cold or with ice cubes and have bowls of relish on the table. These should include chopped mint, toasted pine kernels, fine chopped red peppers and chopped green olives.

Borsch

This clear ruby soup gains from being drunk from good-sized breakfast cups, with an intake of air at the same time, just as a winebiber would and for the same reason: the aeration adds extra flavour.

Makes 8 cups or 6 soup plates
*2 pints (1.1 litres) beef stock or 2 tins consommé
  and 1 pint (570 ml) water*
¾ lb (340 g) young beetroots
*1–2 oz (30–55 g) dried mushrooms (ceps or porcini
  are best)*
2 cloves garlic
½ lb (225 g) onions
2 stalks celery
*salt, bright pepper (see p. 167) and lemon juice
  to taste*

Scrub and cut the beetroot into ½ in (12.5 mm) cubes, quarter the onions and split the garlic. Put all vegetables in the stock and simmer slowly until the beet cubes are a lighter colour than the soup: about 30–40 minutes.

Remove heat from the soup quickly, by standing the pan in cold water, since the colour is fugitive to heat. Strain and season. When ready, reheat but don't boil and add lemon juice at the end if needed. This soup should be bright crimson and crystal clear. It is delicious cold too.

Variation

For a more substantial soup, grate, do not cube, the beetroot; chop the other ingredients so that they will fit on a soup spoon and serve, unstrained, with soured cream.

Eggs and Cheese

Pancakes

There are as many recipes for pancake batter as there are cooks to fry them. The end product varies from a thick, yeast-risen, bread-like pancake to one so lacy that you can almost see through it.

Basic batter is made from flour, egg and milk blended together. Newly made thin batter thickens the moment it's in a hot pan, making it almost impossible to produce a thin pancake. So, in a perfect world, batter should mature and thicken for an hour before it is thinned down to a final pouring thickness. The liquid used for this can be water, milk, thin cream, yoghurt, orange juice, beer or cider. It could be even diluted rum, whisky, brandy or whatever else takes your fancy.

Almost any flour can be used. Self-raising flour puts bubbles in the pancakes making them light and puffy; the whipped whites of egg will do the same temporarily – add them to batter at the last minute before frying begins. Eggs in batter soften the pancake; too many eggs make a batter so 'short' that a pancake will handle more like an omelette. A thick batter makes a thick stodgy pancake. Thin batter makes pancakes too delicate to toss – which is fine if you have two frying pans on the go.

So much for the basic rules. The following recipe is self-lubricating, by which I mean that the first greasing of the pan is the only one.

Thereafter, there will be sufficient butter liberated from the batter by frying to grease the next pancake, which saves time and improves the taste.

Makes 16, thin, 6 in (15 cm)-diameter pancakes
6 oz (170 g) self-raising flour
2 egg whites
3 egg yolks
¾ pint (425 ml) milk or water (or half water and half milk)
2 oz (55 g) butter
salt and sugar (all batters should have both salt and sugar added to improve their taste but not in equal quantities: a hefty pinch or two of sugar and just a small pinch of salt are needed for sweet pancakes, vice versa for savoury ones)

Blend all the ingredients together except the butter. Rest the batter for an hour or so to let it mature, then melt the butter and beat it into the batter. The batter should be the thickness of fresh whipping cream for regular pancakes and single cream for lacy, thin ones. Thicken the mix with more flour if the pancake is too thin to hold together; dilute with water if it can be used to sole shoes.

A thick, heavy pancake means that either the batter is too thick or too much batter has been used. Experiment by using a ladle or two tablespoons of batter and adjust the quantity for subsequent pancakes accordingly. Fry using two pans. The technique of frying pancakes is dealt with fully on pp. 62–3.

Frozen pancakes

Pancakes can be made ahead, layered with cling film, frozen and reheated without losing any of their charm. Reheat them straight from the freezer, by refrying them on one side only (frying one side of a flabby pancake is enough to restore a crisp freshness – frying both sides dries out the pancake too much). Using frozen pancakes makes the production of an impressive dish like crêpe Suzette a matter of minutes. They can also be used as wrappings around all sorts of savoury and sweet fillings. Most of these can be prepared well ahead of serving time – an extra plus.

Sweet Polish pancakes

Make pancakes as above

1 lb (450 g) curd cheese or the Italian curd cheese,
  Ricotta
1 small egg
1 oz (30 g) vanilla sugar
2–3 oz (55–85 g) sultanas
pinch of mace and salt

Sieve the curd cheese to break up the curd. This is easily done using your thumb to press the curd through the mesh. Do have a care if you are tempted to use a processor for this, it is frighteningly easy to beat the texture right out of the curd. Although not disastrous, this would be a shame – its grainy quality is part of the enjoyment. Beat in the small egg, vanilla sugar (or plain sugar and a couple of drops of pure vanilla extract – not vanilla essence, its taste is so false), the sultanas, fresh ground mace and salt.

Spread the pancakes with the filling, roll them up and place them side by side in a grill-proof pan, with the loose side and ends tucked underneath to prevent them unfolding. Sprinkle with sugar and grill until nicely brown. Keep warm until needed. Serve with soured cream (or a mixture of half yoghurt and half whipped cream and the merest pinch of salt).

I soak the sultanas in lemon juice or rum, but you can use whatever takes your fancy by way of alcohol. Add a few curls of lemon or orange zest to the curd for the odd surprise.

Savoury filled pancakes

Make pancakes as above

1 lb (450 g) of mushrooms, made into duxelles
  (see p. 131)
4 oz (115 g) bacon
4 oz (115 g) sweet red peppers
½ pint (285 ml) béchamel sauce (or half béchamel
  and half cream)
2–3 oz (55–85 g) fresh breadcrumbs
1–2 oz (30–55 g) Parmesan, grated

Cut the peppers into cubes the size of a pea and grill quickly until the skins bubble and char. Chop the bacon and grill until crisp. Mix duxelles, crisp bacon and charred peppers and spread onto the pancakes. Roll these up and place in a dish, moisten with béchamel sauce and/or cream, cover with fresh breadcrumbs, then with Parmesan. Put in a medium hot oven until warmed through – about 10–15 minutes – then brown under a grill. Or they can be grilled first and kept in a warm oven until needed, which, from a host's point of view, will probably be more convenient.

Blinis

The pancake part of this Russian speciality has the same ingredients as the basic pancake recipe given above, except that more salt is added and a third of the flour is exchanged for buckwheat flour. No need to buy this flour specially if you have buckwheat to hand, as a coffee grinder will do the job.

I make blinis in either of two ways. After exchanging a third of the flour for buckwheat flour, add 1–2 oz (30–55 g) of yeast to the batter, which, if it is kept warm and given time to work well and smell yeasty, produces a rather thicker, slightly sour pancake with a tender charm so fleeting that the first serving needs to be enjoyed before the next is fried. The second way is to keep the batter on the liquid side, without the yeast, and make very thin pancakes which are much less fragile and can stand around, in warm piles, for half an hour or so. The flavour of the pancake will be authentic if the buckwheat has been roasted – it mostly is these days.

Blinis need to be served warm, on hot plates in the winter, with the thickest sour cream, slightly salted, and plenty of smoked salmon, cut into ¼ in (6 mm) strips. Lemon quarters, fresh dill and a peppermill on the table are desirable extras.

Any thin blinis not eaten can be layered with cling film and stored in the freezer. They can be refreshed from the frozen state by frying quickly on one side only.

Oyster soufflé

Serves 4

Using the cheese soufflé (p. 46) as a base, lightly poach 4 fresh oysters (frozen oysters can be used here without detriment) and use the juice from them in the making of the béchamel. Blend the oysters into the béchamel and add paprika, black pepper and lemon juice to taste. For a surprise, another poached oyster can be added, unblended, half way through the filling of each ramekin. Use about half of the cheese used in the basic recipe.

Garlic soufflé

Serves 4

Follow the cheese soufflé recipe (p. 46), but use cream rather than milk and add two whole heads of garlic, poached until soft (the micro is good for this), peeled and puréed. Bake in a shallow dish (I use an oval one 2 in/5 cm deep by 12 in/30 cm long) with an oven temperature of 230°C/450°F/Gas Mark 8. After 10 minutes push in a skewer; if it comes out clean, or nearly so, it is done.

Toasted or stewed cheese

I first encountered this attention-seeking way of making Welsh rarebit in a lovely old chop house called Simpsons up an alleyway off Cornhill in the City of London. At that time, women's lib had hardly dawned in Chelsea let alone in the male stronghold of the City, and the polished brass hat racks between the communal pews were full of bowlers and umbrellas, with never a pretty face in sight. As in its more famous namesake in the Strand, the centre of attention was the trolley laden with the roast of the day. The old girls who used to serve in this den were familiar with their regulars and, without finesse, gave a rapid rough and ready service laced with plenty of backchat. Things hadn't changed since Edwardian times. So, what was this 'Stewed Cheese' on the rather sticky menu? A pot of melted cheese with a thick brown crust and finger toast to dip into it. A minute afterwards a bottle of Lea & Perrins would arrive, unasked for, to spike up more jaded palates. Heaven! Washed down with beer drawn from the wood this confection lives with me still.

Serves 4
5 oz (140 g) of béchamel sauce (see p. 130)
5 oz (140 g) of well-matured Cheddar cheese
1 level teaspoon mustard powder
1 teaspoon of Worcestershire sauce
salt and pepper to taste
4 ramekins (3 in/7.5 cm diameter by 1½ in/4 cm deep)

Warm the béchamel sauce and melt into it an equal quantity of matured Cheddar cheese. Add a level teaspoon of mustard powder (some like less but I think it needs at least that, especially if the only mustard to hand is ready-made out of jar), pepper and salt to taste. I find that Worcestershire sauce is essential for this dish but some people can live without it – about 1 teaspoon of Lea & Perrins for old times' sake then. Load the mixture into ramekins and heat slowly in an oven or microwave. Put under a grill until nicely brown. If ramekins are a problem serve it in a communal bowl, nice and shallow for maximum browning and flavour. Serve with grissini or finger toast piled on a separate plate. Eating it this way is very *fondue*, which suggests a cross-pollination: take it easy on the mustard and make the béchamel with white wine. Another finesse is to sprinkle dried herb (thyme is good) on the crust to burn with the browning. If the cheese is immature and lacks bite, add a splash of vinegar, and maybe a drop of Tabasco.

Choux pastry

This is the basic filler in quite a number of dishes. It is flexible since it can be poached (for dumplings), steamed (for gnocchi), baked (for éclairs) and fried (for doughnuts).

4 oz (115 ml) water
2 oz (55 g) butter
2½ oz (70 g) flour
2 eggs
½ teaspoon salt and a good pinch each of pepper
*   and mace*

Boil the water and butter in a saucepan, beat in the flour and continue beating until the mixture is smooth. Add seasoning. With the pan off the heat, add the eggs. All this beating can be done in a food processor in about 2 minutes, but the water and butter have to be hot enough to thicken the flour, so I think using a saucepan is safer.

Potato gnocchi

Make the basic choux pastry recipe above and mix with an equal quantity of mashed potato, re-season and add 1 oz (30 g) of grated Parmesan. Shape into 3 in (8 cm) sausages and poach in gently simmering, salty water for 15–20 minutes, when they should be almost twice their original diameter. Or, if you have a piping bag, fit it with an ½ in (1.25 cm) nozzle, cut off ½ in (1.25 cm) pieces with a wet knife straight into the poaching water.

Serve with a creamy sauce as a starter; or paint them with garlic oil, dust with Parmesan and grill brown to serve with a main course; or freeze for another day. This recipe is adaptable: potato can be replaced by cooked couscous (semolina) or soaked bulgar to vary the texture, and they can be deep-fried in almost smoking hot oil instead of poaching.

Spinach gnocchi with anchovy cream

Anchovy cream

Cut up anchovy fillets into peppercorn size pieces, or use best quality anchovy purée from a tube, and stir into whipping cream with a little garlic oil. Colour pink with tomato purée for maximum colour contrast. I find that four or five fillets will flavour 10 oz (285 ml) of cream quite nicely.

Gnocchi

Make the basic choux pastry recipe above and mix it with an equal weight of cooked spinach; add 1 oz (30 g) of grated Parmesan and season with fresh ground mace. Poach as above. Serve, well drained, with anchovy cream.

Éclairs and profiteroles

Using a 1½ in (4 cm) nozzle in a piping bag, pipe 'sausages' (éclairs) or balls (profiteroles) of choux, onto a baking tray and bake in a hot oven (220°C/425°F/Gas Mark 7) until they are golden brown, about 20 minutes. Pierce their sides with a skewer and cool. Fill the hollow insides with whipped sweetened cream flavoured with a sweet liqueur and top with melted chocolate. An interesting variation is to use strong black coffee instead of water in the basic recipe.

Make savoury versions by adding cheese to the choux (1 part cheese to 2 parts choux) and filling with a savoury cream. One of the creams I use is puréed smoked fish combined with butter, fresh ground pepper and a squeeze of lemon.

Crostini

Mix choux pastry with an equal quantity of well-flavoured, minced cooked ham, or prawns, or grated Parmesan, and a fresh herb. Spread on toast, well insulated from moisture with garlic oil (see p. 165), and bake in a hot oven (220°C/425°F/Gas Mark 8) until they are nicely puffed up, about 15 minutes. Cut into bite-sized pieces to serve as canapés.

Microwaved scrambled eggs

These scrambled eggs differ from those made in a saucepan in that they can be made to have more lightness and bulk. Small parts of the egg mixture get overcooked in the microwave and become fluffy, but the overall succulence – its juiciness – doesn't suffer on the way. And when eggs are microwaved, they seem to be able to absorb more butter than in conventional cooking, so that they can be made really rich but light.

Take two eggs per person, or five for three – it's one of those sort of dishes – crack them into a basin and season to taste. Apart from the usual salt and pepper, I like the merest hint of fresh ground mace and a small pinch of

MSG, which gives a 'fresh egg' taste to the dish. Add a teaspoon of liquid per egg – milk, cream, water or even white wine with caution – and the same amount of butter, then beat with a fork, not too much as a little obvious egg white looks attractive in the final dish. Microwave in the basin until the edges of the mixture begin to set and froth. This can happen quite quickly, so start to keep a watchful eye after 30 seconds. Take out the basin and stir in the firmed edges. If you have been neglectful, the edges will need not only stirring in but breaking up into small pieces – large pieces of set froth are dry to the palate and are as unpleasant in scrambled eggs as they are in an overcooked soufflé. Continue to stir in the edges, as they form, until there seems to be more set than unset egg.

Now is a good time to butter the toast while the residual heat in the eggs carries on with the cooking. Give the mixture a final stir and assess if the eggs are creamy enough. If not, add a little more cream or butter. I add a raw egg yolk if the eggs seem dry and are still hot enough to cook it a little. The raw egg has a good mouth texture with a splendid after-taste, just right for scrambled eggs.

If you have an urge to add a green herb, use fresh tarragon or dill but not too much. These eggs have a delicate taste which is easily lost.

Shellfish

Grilled oysters

Allow 3–5 oysters (according to size) per person for a substantial starter.

Open the oysters, deep shell down to preserve the juice, and leave them in the deep half shell. Season fresh breadcrumbs with salt and pepper and mix half and half with freshly grated Parmesan. Dribble a half teaspoon of garlic oil and a small squeeze of lemon juice over each oyster then cover with a generous sprinkle of seasoned breadcrumbs. Put in a flat dish – a frying pan will be fine – and brown under a medium grill, or some distance away from a hot grill. The grilling should be slow enough to allow for some heat to set the oysters before the topping has finished browning.

A less flamboyant, but almost as delicious, variation is made with mussels.

Grilled mussels

Allow 6–8 mussels per person.

Scrub the shells then lightly poach the mussels; they should be removed from the lightly salted boiling water immediately they open, singly if necessary. Use a frying pan for poaching, as it is easier, with a single layer of mussels, to see which have opened. Leave each mussel on its half shell with a drop of juice. Proceed as for oysters but under a hotter grill, the mussels are cooked already and don't want overcooking.

Stir-fried king prawns

Allow 5–6 prawns per person as a starter.

This dish requires a supply of raw, frozen king prawns. These have their shells on but their heads off. Find them in a Chinese super-market freezer, where there are usually several sizes, I use those which weigh 20 to the lb (450 g).

Defrost the prawns in hot, well-salted

water – a micro will accelerate this process considerably. Squeeze a prawn to see how squidgy a raw one feels to have a point of comparison with when they are cooked and firm.

In a large frying pan, or a wok, pour a generous dessertspoon of garlic oil (see p. 165) and a level teaspoon of fine-chopped fresh chilli, seeds and all. Brown the chilli in the oil, then put in some of the prawns, well drained. Stir or toss steadily over the fiercest heat until all the blue shells have turned an appetizing red/pink, then squeeze one to check if they are done. If it has the same firmness all along it should be OK. If the prawns start to give off some of their juice, they are definitely done if not overdone. To make absolutely sure, peel and eat one at the range.

Keep the first batch warm while the process is repeated with the remainder. How many prawns you can fry successfully at one time rather depends on how much heat you have at your disposal. Slow frying allows the prawns to cook through – and start to lose their body fluid – before the shells go opaque and brown at the edges. Better to fry a small quantity fiercely, allowing the prawns to retain their juices, than fry more and risk them getting stewed in their own juice – not a bad fate but hardly stir-frying.

Although there is plenty of chilli on the shell, the prawn inside is not affected; if you like chilli, suck your fingers clean, if not – don't. Provide finger bowls at table and have a disposable napkin to hand.

Fish

Court-bouillon for poaching fish

You can poach a fish in plain, salted water or
you can steam it. And if the fish is very fresh
(such a rare occurrence for most of us), it would
be a shame not to poach it. But usually a fish
needs a little help and to poach it in a court-
bouillon gives just the sort of lift that will
make the eating of it memorable.

3 pints (1.7 litres) water
1 pint (570 ml) dry white wine
3 sticks of celery
2 leeks
½ head of garlic
3 medium-sized carrots
handful of parsley or chervil (or other anise-
  flavoured herb)
5 bay leaves
5 juniper berries, crushed
1 level dessertspoon each of salt and peppercorns
1 teaspoon of sugar
zest of ½ lemon

Boil this collation for half an hour and strain.

Poached salmon

Have enough bouillon to cover the fish and
bring it to a rolling boil in a fish kettle. Introduce a gutted salmon – with its head on but
with the gills removed to keep the bouillon
sweet – and bring the bouillon back to the boil

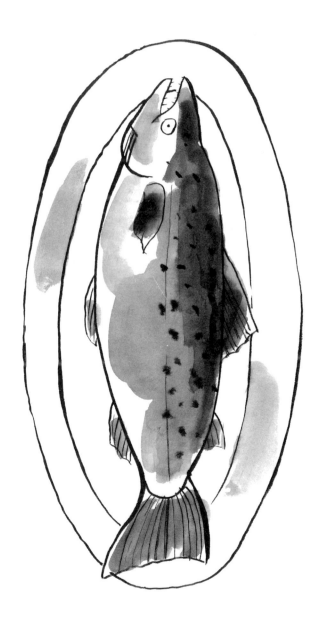

for a couple of minutes. Remove the kettle from the heat and let the fish stand in the bouillon for half an hour, or until you need it. By this time the heat will have suffused to the fish's backbone. I find that it is unnecessary to serve poached fish piping hot; on the contrary, the flavour is improved by it being just warm. Strain off the bouillon and serve the fish on hot plates as this stops the juices congealing.

Strain the bouillon for another day and keep it well wrapped in the freezer. When poaching more fish, refresh the bouillon with new pot herbs and it will continue to improve and make succeeding fish yet more tasty. The classic sauce for poached fish is hollandaise (see p. 131).

Dover sole à la meunière

The fresher the fish, the better it tastes. This golden rule has its exception, like any other, and one exception is Dover sole – the prince of flat fish. Dover sole is a very firm fish, so firm that, when it is really fresh, it is impossible to skin without pulling away small divots of flesh with the skin. After a bit of relaxing deterioration it can be skinned cleanly, and the flavour improves. A minimum of 2–3 days is needed for the full flavour to develop. The fishermen of Folkestone Harbour, where I used to buy my fish fresh off the trawler, thought it a waste of a good fish to eat it immature. Although this recipe is for Dover sole, any firm fish can be fried in this way.

Trim the fish of its fins and remove its coarse black skin. Dab the fish dry with a paper towel and dust with seasoned flour.

Melt 3 oz (85 g) of unsalted butter in a saucepan and pour off the clear butterfat into a frying pan large enough to allow the fish to lie flat, keeping the curds for later.

Heat the pan on medium heat until the fat begins to ripple and lay in the fish skinned side down. Fry until the surface is golden brown, then, using two spatulas to keep the fish in good shape, turn the fish over to brown the other side. Remove the fish from the pan to a warm place and wipe out the pan with a paper towel to remove the burnt bits.

Add 1 oz (30 g) of salted butter and the reserved curds from the clarifying to the pan and gently fry until they are pale nut brown. Squeeze in some lemon juice, a little fresh ground pepper and, just before serving, add some chopped parsley; then pour this golden and green sauce over the browned fish.

How the recipe works

Clarifying the butter removes the curds that brown and blacken in such an unsightly way before the fish has a chance to take colour.

Heat degenerates some of the gelatinous connecting tissue in the flesh and releases body fluids at the same time and these juices will glue the fish to the pan given half a chance. Dover sole has less body fluid than other flat fish and so that makes it less likely to stick, but even then it is a distinct hazard. It helps if the pan is a non-stick one and is kept moving –

a jiggle at frequent intervals should do the trick. And it is good if the frying is fast enough to complete the browning before the flesh is cooked through, since there will be less fluid released. A warm resting place can be used to complete the cooking while the sauce is made.

Even with gentle heating, the curds in the sauce can overbrown all too easily. Fortunately, once the curds are a nice colour, adding lemon juice takes the heat out of the sauce and stops further browning.

Adding the parsley just before serving, stops it losing its green in the acidity.

It is easy to see why this dish has become famous. Apart from the flavour of the fish itself, there is the crisp texture of the fried flesh and its succulent juices; the browned butter adds a toasted nut flavour, while the lemon juice neatly cuts its richness. It is also easy to see why it isn't served much at home. The fish needs serving pretty quickly while it still has a firm texture and a crisp skin; and for it to be kept waiting while another fish is cooked is almost too long to wait – unless, of course, you have two pans.

Salting and Marinating Fish

Short-term pickling of fish is practised on both sides of the Atlantic and it is interesting to compare the Norwegian gravadlax with the Mexican cebiche. They are quite different methods: one relying on salt, the other on acid to make them palatable.

Gravadlax

This calls for a mixture of equal parts of sugar and salt, spiked with pepper and freshened with plenty of chopped dill. Apply this to both sides of each fillet of fish – salmon in this case – and lay them face to face. Put them under a weight and leave for not less than a day, and not more than four, in the fridge. Slice thinly and serve with a sauce. Make this from mayonnaise, French or German mustard, enough white wine or wine vinegar to make it pourable and enough dill to make it pale green. Treat filleted herrings in the same way (but using something more robust than the delicately flavour dill – lovage or parsley, for instance) before turning them into pickled herrings or roll-mops.

Cebiche

This pickle is more immediate in its action, taking about six hours to 'cook' the fish, and is nothing more than pure, fresh lime juice, lightly salted.

Serves 4
1 lb (450 g) fish – salmon or any firm, white fish
6 limes
½ teaspoon salt
1 tablespoon oil
salt, pepper and sugar to taste
10 oz (285 g) tomatoes
¼ in (6 mm) chilli
pinch of dried basil
2–3 spring onions, sliced

Cut the fish into ½ in (12 mm) cubes, roll in salted lime juice until they become opalescent and cooked-looking. Add the rest of the marinade, or vinaigrette as I prefer to think of it – that is the oil, pepper, a pinch of sugar and a bit more salt perhaps. Add sliced tomatoes, a good pinch of dried basil and fine-chopped chilli to taste. Rest for an hour, add thin sliced spring onions and there it is.

Other pickling methods

There are other ways of using pickle to flavour rather than 'cook' the fish.

Escabèche This is where the fish is fried first before being put in the equivalent of a vinaigrette with onions and herbs for a few hours to pick up the flavour.

Soused fish Here the fish is simmered, or put into a low oven, in a marinade of dilute vinegar or wine and seasoning. If the fish is small, it is sufficient to put it in a hot marinade.

Meat and Poultry

Fricadelles

Fricadelles is the Scandinavian word for minced pork meat balls and I prefer it to other names in other tongues. This version differs somewhat from the fricadelles I had in Stockholm.

Serves 6
1 lb (450 g) minced pork
1 lb (450 g) best sausage meat
2 tablespoons garlic oil
1 lb (450 g) onions

Seasoning
$\frac{1}{2}$ *chilli, fine-chopped*
1 dessertspoon coriander seed, freshly ground
2 teaspoons mace, freshly ground
2 teaspoons hot paprika (smoked, if you can
*   get it)*
1 rounded tablespoon fresh, smoky-flavoured
*   herb, chopped (sage or thyme is perfect)*
zest and juice of 1 lemon

Peel and finely chop the onions (I use a food processor for this quantity) and fry in the garlic oil until they begin to brown. Add to the minced pork and sausagemeat and mix well with the rest of the ingredients.

Add as much stock (browned boned for preference, see p. 95) as the meat will take and still hold its shape when formed into balls – in other words pretty slack. Check the seasoning by frying a small piece – if it needs salt, and it probably will, use soya sauce.

Form into golf balls and put into a shallow baking dish (one with shallow sides will allow the heat to brown the tops of the fricadelles), dress with any excess oil and put into a medium oven, half way up the heat scale, for half an hour. If the tops aren't brown, raise the oven shelf until they are. When the fricadelles are giving off juice they are done. Put this juice into a sharp hot tomato sauce and serve with the fricadelles. When fully baked, the water content evaporates and leaves these balls light, moist and delicately crumbly. Eat hot, but they are also good cold.

Hot tomato sauce

Fry a little red paprika in garlic oil, add fresh tomato purée and enough vinegar to make it interesting. Add the pan juices and blend together.

Other uses

Make fricadelles the size of large grapes and freeze. These can be fried straight from the freezer and, if you like them, should be considered as an essential part of the shortcuts store cupboard. Use them, browned, in a pasta sauce or to turn a vegetable soup starter into a main course.

For a Chinese slant, change the seasoning to fresh ginger finely chopped, add loads of fresh green coriander or basil but keep the chopped fresh chilli and lemon.

Two-way duck

A 4–5 lb (1.8–2.3 kg) duck is enough for 4 people.

Remove the breasts, keeping their skins on, and freeze them. Remove the legs and make a rich stock from the rest. Strain the stock and lightly poach the legs in it until the flesh on them is just loose enough to strip from the bone. Remove legs from the stock, and reduce it to half the volume (or more, you'll need about half a pint (285 ml) of gravy), skim off the fat and adjust for salt. Add something sharp and sweet – this could be a Seville orange or a lemon, chopped small and cooked in the gravy until soft (black cherries are very good in season but add them stoned *just* before serving, which will keep them juicy and firm). Cut the leg meat small and replace in the gravy.

This gravy can be kept in the fridge for two or three days, or it can be frozen without spoiling for a week or more. As the rest of the preparation takes no more than half an hour, this dish could easily become an impressive 'shortcut' dish.

Remove the breasts from the freezer, wait until the skin is soft enough to score but the flesh is frozen hard still. Score the skin with cuts $\frac{1}{4}$ in (6 mm) apart and down to the flesh. Rub salt into the cuts. Grill the skin crisp and brown and put in a moderate oven until the breasts are cooked pink. Slice thinly, each slice with its own piece of crisp skin, and serve on a pool of stew.

This recipe is good not only for duck but for all poultry, suitably adjusted of course – only duck and goose have skin thick enough for crisping.

Chicken in aspic

This is a dish that makes a feature on buffet tables or is nice as a cold starter. It is simplicity itself.

Simmer a chicken for an hour with pot herbs and herbs in a tincture of half white wine and half salted water. Take off the breast and leg meat and brown the rest in a hot oven. Keep the crisp skin and return the rest to the stock with two whole garlic bulbs (their tops and tails sliced off). Simmer for half an hour. Keep the chicken fat to fry potatoes in and the crisp skin to serve, chopped, over mashed potatoes or boiled rice.

Clarify the stock (see p. 95), reinforcing it with chicken glaze cubes from the freezer (see p. 162) or condensed consommé from a tin.

Stiffen with gelatine if necessary – it should have the consistency of table jelly when cool. Taste for stimulants – have it stronger in acid and salt than you would think, the flavour of the aspic is diluted by the additions to come. Don't forget that a pinch of sugar might be a good idea. Adjust the acidity with lemon juice.

Chop the cold meat into bite-sized pieces, add a tablespoon or two of chopped fresh tarragon or parsley, quite coarse. Tarragon is the traditional herb, so use that if you have it. Use whole sprigs of the herb, blanched, in the decoration. Add lemon zest to taste. Squeeze out the cloves from the garlic bulbs; slice and dry two or three pickled gherkins, and all that is left is the assembly.

The mould can be whatever shape takes your fancy; a shallow one will make it easier to serve in pretty portions. Make individual moulds or ramekins for a sit-down meal.

Pour the melted aspic into the mould. Leave to cool until there is a $\frac{1}{8}$ in (3 mm) layer set onto the mould. This setting is a deal faster if the mould is sitting in some cold water. Pour off the fluid aspic into a bowl containing all the other ingredients except the decorating herb.

Arrange the blanched herb onto the aspic lining. Give the bowl a stir and pour the contents into the mould, gently, so as not to disturb the liner or the arranged herb. When it is nearly set, sprinkle paprika all over the top to give a coloured base when the mould is inverted. Warm the mould until the aspic is liberated but not melted; then place the serving dish over the mould and overturn it.

Hot chicken salad

Serves 4
4 medium-sized chicken breasts (I buy whole chickens for the price of the breasts, taking off the breasts and leg meat and using the remainder for good chicken stock)
$\frac{1}{2}$ lb (225 g) thin green beans
2–3 roots of coriander (enough to yield around a dozen 2 in/5 cm stalks)
$\frac{3}{4}$ oz (20 g) almonds

Marinade
1 tablespoon light soy sauce
1 tablespoon lemon juice
zest of $\frac{1}{2}$ lemon
$1\frac{1}{2}$ oz (45 g) fresh ginger, grated
1–2 teaspoons garlic oil
1 teaspoon fresh chilli (optional), chopped
1 teaspoon sugar

Skin the breasts (the leg meat too if you want more), and put them into the marinade for at least two hours. If the marinating is to be done overnight, don't make the pickle too sharp or salty as it will drown the chicken taste. Trim and blanch the green beans and the coriander stalks (see p. 52 on blanching). Blanch the almonds of their skins and, for perfection, split them in half before frying (see p. 140).

Take the breasts from the marinade, dab them dry, dust with flour and fry brown on one side and lightly brown on the other, using garlic oil. Keep them in a warm oven, to finish cooking, until ready to serve.

Check whether the breasts are cooked or not by pressing each breast – press with a finger – for resilience. The difference between cooked flesh and uncooked is one of firmness, and as the thin end will certainly be cooked, you'll be able to tell if that firmness is continual all the way along. Another way is to ease up the fillet, found on the underside of the breast, and see if the flesh exposed is pink at all. If it is, take off this fillet and fry both pink sides – of the fillet and the underside – in the pan for a minute or two. This will not ruin the final effect as the breasts are to be sliced anyway. I prefer to have the breast meat juicy rather than drily overdone; it's better to err on the underdone side, when it can be so easily corrected.

When the breasts are ready to serve, put the beans and stalks into the frying pan and give them a quick stir-fry to heat them up and coat them with oil. Remove these from the pan and introduce the marinade, which can be reduced by frying to strengthen the taste or diluted with white wine if it is too strong. Add a teaspoonful of arrowroot or cornflour mixed with water to give the sauce a clinging gloss and emulsify the oil. Give this liaison a quick rolling boil to make it clear and glossy, toss the beans and stalks in this sauce and place them on a serving dish with the sliced juicy breast meat lying in the middle of the dish (its browned edges will show to nice effect against the white flesh). Sprinkle with coriander leaves, four-spice powder (see p. 167) and the almonds. Serve with boiled rice or rice noodles made fragrant with cardamom.

Make a ginger relish to pass around after the first mouthful or two.

Fresh ginger relish

With a sharp knife cut the thinnest ever slices
of fresh young ginger; cut along the grain not
across it. Pile up these slices and cut again to
produce fine slivers of ginger half a matchstick
thick. Put these in wine vinegar, salted with
soy sauce and slightly sweetened, for no longer
than half an hour.

Pekinese-style chicken

Basically this dish is slices of crisp-skinned
roast chicken served with pancakes and several
relishes and sauces. The chicken slices are
placed on a pancake and dressed with relish;
the pancake is then rolled up and eaten by
hand, which produces a charming chatty infor-
mality as well as an extra textural pleasure.

Serves 4
3½ lb (1.6 kg) oven-ready chicken (for each extra
  person increase weight by ½ lb/225 g)
2½ pints (1.4 litres) of brine (2½ oz/70 g salt for
  every pint/570 ml of water)
2 teaspoons four-spice powder (see p. 167 or use
  the commercial five-spice powder)
2 tablespoons garlic oil (see p. 165)

Pancakes
11 oz (310 g) plain or self-raising flour
12 fl oz (340 ml) water, near boiling

Cover the chicken with brine for 1–2 hours,
drain and dry.

Introduce four-spice powder between the
skin and the flesh of the chicken. To do this
ease a finger under the skin round the outside
of the thighs and over the breast (see p. 40 if
you're uncertain what I mean). Hang the
carcass in a windy place, or in front of an

electric fan or fan heater set on cold, until the
skin is paper dry. Paint with garlic oil and
lightly sprinkle with more four-spice powder.
Put the bird in a shallow-sided tray, on its side,
so that one breast rests on the tray, and put it
into a hot oven (220°C/425°F/Gas Mark 6).
Cook until sizzling can be heard (about 15
minutes), turn the bird onto its other breast,
baste with oil from the tray or extra garlic oil,
prick any skin blisters, reduce the temperature
to moderate (180°C/350°F/Gas Mark 4) and cook
for about 40 minutes.

Turn up the heat (220°C/425°F/Gas Mark 7), turn the bird breast side up, lightly dredge it with seasoned flour, add a squeeze of lemon to the juices in the pan, prick and baste, sprinkle with a little icing sugar and return to the oven. Baste at regular intervals until the skin is nicely brown with a sheen – 10–15 minutes should be enough. Allow about $1\frac{1}{4}$ – $1\frac{1}{2}$ hours in all. For birds over $3\frac{1}{2}$ lbs (1.6 g), add 15 minutes per extra lb (450 g) at the lower temperature. After cooking, it does the chicken no harm at all to rest in a warm place for 20 minutes.

Carve the bird into pieces the size of a young girl's finger. Put back any soft skin from the carcass into the top of the oven for a brief final crisping. Roll the chicken pieces in the pan juices with a squeeze more lemon and keep them warm in the bottom of the oven, while the accompanying pancakes are finished.

Pancakes

Unlike pancakes which are made from batter and get their shape from the frying pan, these are made from dough and get their shape by rolling. Mix the flour with the near-boiling water, beating well. Roll the dough into a long sausage on a well-floured board and divide into 24 pieces. Form these into flat cakes 2 in (5 cm) in diameter. Oil one side of a cake, press another onto it and roll this duplex out to a 6 in (15 cm) double pancake. Heat in a lightly greased pan on low heat for about 1–2 minutes per side – a lid will stop them drying out while this is going on. Keep them warm while cooking the rest, then separate pancake in half. Serve in a pile to keep them warm and pliable.

Side Dishes

Serve hoisin sauce, either bottled or make your own by mashing together until smooth 3 parts of fermented yellow beans, 2 parts honey, 1 part each of toasted sesame and fresh garlic oil; dilute with lemon juice. Bottled hoisin is vinegary and tastes artificial in the way that most manufactured sauces do.

Spring onions are a traditional accompaniment: cut them into 2 in (5 cm) lengths and into thin slivers lengthwise. They will curl up prettily in less than an hour if plunged into iced water; the thinner the strips, the curlier the slivers become.

Matchstick strips of cucumber, which provide freshness and crunch, and lightly salted shreds of crisp chicken skin, are also served with this dish.

Serving

To serve, take a pancake and assemble in it a few shreds of crisp skin, fingers of juicy chicken, onion slivers, cucumber strips and the sauce. Fold up one end to stop the juices running out and eat from the other end – a textural banquet.

Two or three pancakes of this combination seems to me to be enough and then another flavour is called for. This could be a ginger relish made from slivers of fresh ginger, cut as thin as you can along the grain and soaked for half an hour in salty vinegar; fresh grated horseradish served with a spoon; a relish of chopped tomato, fine chopped flesh of a chilli and salt; lemon chutney (see p. 138); or whatever takes your fancy. In order to stop an extra relish being used at the beginning, reserve it, off table, until you are ready for a change.

Variations

This dish is nice with rice or soft noodles instead of pancakes but the textural satisfaction of using fingertips is lost.

Substitute roast pork for chicken. Cut belly pork, without the rind, into 2 in (5 cm) cubes, dust with four-spice powder and icing sugar and roast slowly (about 1½ hours at 150°C/300°F/Gas Mark 2) until the fat is brown and crunchy, then cut into thin slices. Of course, if you have mastered the art of making fine crackling, that would be splendid with this dish.

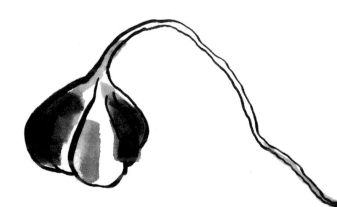

Cantonese-style chicken

Serves 4
3½ lb (1.6 kg) oven-ready chicken (for every extra person increase weight by ½ lb/225 g)
2½ pints (1.4 litres) of brine (2½ oz/70 g salt for every pint/570 ml of water)
a good handful of coriander leaves (keep the stalks for later), chopped

Basting mixture
1 tablespoon each of sherry, honey, concentrated tomato purée, lemon juice and light soy sauce
1 tablespoon coarse-cut marmalade
1 in (2.5 cm) fresh ginger root in shreds
2 cloves garlic, sliced thinly
garlic oil

Brine the chicken, as for Peking chicken above, and introduce the fresh chopped coriander under the skin (see p. 40 for more on this). Paint the skin with garlic oil. Put the bird in a shallow-sided tray, on its side, so that one breast rests on the tray. Put the bird into a hot oven (220°C/425°F/Gas Mark 6) and cook until sizzling can be heard (about 15 minutes). Paint all the skin with the basting mixture. Turn the bird onto its other breast, reduce the temperature to moderate (180°C/350°F/Gas Mark 4) and cook for about 45 minutes. Keep an eye on the browning of the 'paint', it burns easily.

Turn the bird on its back, with both breasts showing, and roast for 20 minutes more. Baste frequently during this time, with pan juices and basting mixture alternately, until it is nicely brown all over. For a special Chinese touch, sprinkle sesame seed all over the sticky skin half way through the browning. When the roasting is complete, a good gloss should have built up on the skin. If it hasn't, turn up the heat and baste regularly until it has.

Carve the bird into pieces that chopsticks can manage and place in the bottom of the oven. Any pieces that could do with more cooking should go in the top while the sauce is prepared.

Make the sauce from the pan juices, the remaining mixture, the marmalade (with as much peel as you can spare, cut up so that everyone will get some), the finely chopped garlic, the shreds of fresh ginger and a handful of fresh coriander stalks – 1 in (2.5 cm) long and matchstick thin. Bring this amalgam to a full rolling boil (thin with sherry and chicken stock if needed) and adjust the seasoning. When doing this, don't just check for sweetness-saltiness, think about acidity and whether a little chilli or MSG (for the *umami* effect) might be a good idea. Don't cook the brightness out of the ginger and garlic or, if you do, add more.

Pour the sauce over the chicken and sprinkle with fresh green herbs. Serve with a dish of boiled noodles, stir-fried with garlic oil and a spoonful of peanut butter (soften the butter in the oil before throwing in the pre-cooked noodles); add soy, lemon zest and chopped spring onions. Consider a side dish of steamed green vegetables, served with a streak of oyster sauce down the centre of the dish and topped with fried cashews.

Roast Chicken Variations

Using the roast chicken recipe in Chapter 4 as a basis (see p. 40), here are a few further variations.

Olive chicken

Use olive purée under the skin. This is available off the shelf in some places but it isn't too difficult to grind your own.

Make the purée from stoned green or black olives steeped in boiling hot water for a minute, repeating if very salty; mash them with a crushed garlic clove and put under the skin. Because the purée is salty, reduce the brining time accordingly. Slice 6–8 garlic cloves and place under the carcass before roasting. These should be nicely browned when the time comes to make the sauce. Blend them into the sauce or leave them whole – cooked garlic lumps are nice to find. Add 1 teaspoon of paprika for colour and finish as in the basic recipe. Add a

teaspoonful of capers to this intense sauce to sharpen the occasional mouthful.

Serve with plain boiled rice coloured with saffron and sweetened with fresh chopped fennel or other aniseed-flavoured green herb (see pp. 86–7). Put lemon chutney (see p. 138) and a tomato salad on the table.

Mushroom chicken

Make a mushroom purée by mashing cultivated and wild mushrooms (fresh or dried) with a couple of crushed garlic cloves, a teaspoon of dried thyme or a tablespoon of fresh thyme in a food processor. Use the flat, open, dark-gilled, cultivated mushrooms with a quarter of the volume of fine-chopped, soaked, dried mushrooms – ceps are the best for this. Check the purée for salt (soy is good here) and pepper. This purée gives the best truffly taste possible without truffles. Put it under the skin as in the basic recipe and use it to flavour the sauce too.

Add a pinch of mace to the purée and thicken it with cream.

Serve with plain noodles made bright with lemon and fresh green herb; this means adding a slurp of white wine and some good olive oil to stop the noodles sticking together after they are cooked, and then adding lemon flesh in small pieces, without pith, and chopped green herb. Introduce a salad during the eating of this dish, to be eaten on the same plate. The sauce on the plate will add richness to the salad and the salad will add crunch to the other textures.

Paprika chicken

After the brining in the basic recipe, add paprika and a little black pepper under the skin and sprinkle more over the oiled skin. Put chopped garlic, 3 or 4 cloves at least, to brown under the bird in the pan before putting it into the oven. Baste more than usual to get a lovely

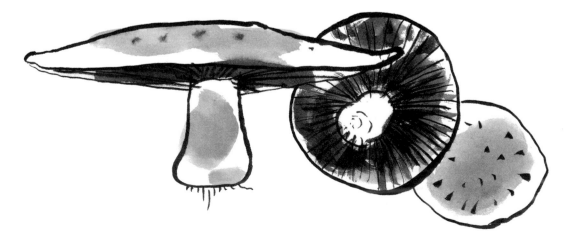

rosy brown skin. Unless piquant paprika is used the sauce will need bolstering with fresh chilli, at least $\frac{1}{2}$ in (1.5 cm) or according to taste. (The heat in chilli, capsaicin, is not so much in the flesh or the seeds but in the lighter-coloured pith that holds the seeds on.) Boil the stock for 30 minutes to allow the heat of the chilli to disperse and produce a hot brightness. Bay leaves (3–5), caraway and/or cumin seeds (up to 1 teaspoon) should also be added to the boiling for an authentic flavour. Proceed as for the basic recipe.

The caraway flavour, so wonderfully complementary to paprika and traditional with this dish, could be added in another way: by frying the seed to a light brown in garlic oil and sprinkling it on the rice or boiled potatoes served with the chicken.

Tomato purée will enhance the colour and thicken the sauce; any separated oil will be orange-red and look pretty. For an interesting variation, thicken the sauce with a little unsweetened chocolate powder; it won't do much for the colour but the depth is profound. Try half a teaspoon to see if you like it first, it's not to everyone's taste. Any of the brighteners mentioned in the basic recipe will be good and needful – this is a rich sauce. With a dish as red as this, a green will be needed to balance the colour – either a load of chopped fresh coriander or other green herb (mint would be nice) sprinkled over the dish, or a pretty green vegetable. This, with the white rice and a segment of lemon, should make the dish a picture.

Variations

This paprika recipe works very nicely with roasted pork, beef or lamb and it is relatively quick too. Cut the meat into 2 in (5 cm) cubes before roasting to have a lot of browned outside meat bolstering the flavour. Rub the surfaces with garlic oil, salt and paprika. Cubes of this size will need a shallow tray and a fast oven to brown if they are not to be overcooked inside, say 220°C/425°F/Gas Mark 7 for 20 minutes or until the meat is sizzling, then down to 160°C/325°F/Gas Mark 3 until it is done; test by cutting one of the cubes in half if necessary. The cubes should be kept warm while the sauce is prepared. Thereafter follow the technique pretty well as for paprika chicken; cut up the cubes into slices – the coarser the grain of the meat, the thinner the slices.

Chicken *mole*

I've mentioned adding unsweetened chocolate powder to paprika chicken, and this Mexican dish goes a stage further. Use more chocolate, less paprika and remember that chilli is needed to balance the 'thick' taste. It is a dish to play around with, everyone has their own idea of how it should taste. It need not be a blockbuster of a dish. Now that I've got used to it, the chocolate/chilli combination is more often used as a mysterious little background something – under a creamy walnut sauce with boiled chicken for instance.

leek

parsnip

asparagus

carrot

turnip

celery

red onion

spring
onion

swede

garlic

Vegetables

Asparagus

These expensive delicacies need special treatment to get the best out of them. The base of the stalk is considerably tougher than the tip, and the way to get the whole stalk cooked perfectly is to cook the bottom third for the full time, the middle for two thirds of the time and the tips for one third of the time. There are several ways of achieving this impossibility. In a fully equipped kitchen there will be a pan deep enough to take the height of the stalks. If that is the case, all that is necessary is to pour boiling, salted water one third of the way up the stalks and cook for a third of the time with a lid on, add more water for another third of the time and cover the tips for the last third of the time. For those with no such pan, here is another method.

Tie the spears into bundles so that they will stand up on their own. Put into the deepest pan you have and cover the protruding tips with a lid made of aluminium foil so that it covers the sides of the pan too (indent this improvised lid so that condensation drops within the pan). In this way the tips only get steamed. That may be enough if the cooking time is on the long side. The total cooking time varies from 9 minutes for the freshest, most tender spears and up to 30–40 minutes for fat white monsters. Be prepared to lose the colour to get them soft and have the full asparagus flavour.

Microwaving in a pool of water under cling-film saves the colour of freshly picked asparagus. When not so fresh, from a shop for instance, they will need soaking well first. Since the cooking goes on at the same rate all over the stalks with a microwave, only by placing the tips towards the centre will they be saved from overcooking. Allow about 4 minutes (up to 6–8 minutes for tougher spears) per pound (0.5 kg). Lay the loose asparagus two or three deep. Test with a needle for tenderness.

The usual sauce to serve with this special vegetable is hollandaise (see p. 131), but if you find it a bit rich, mix it with some whipped cream and a pinch more salt.

Garlicky mushrooms

These are simplicity itself with garlic oil to hand.

Use fresh mushrooms. Allow 3 oz (85 g) per person. Trim the mushroom stalks down to the rim of the mushroom cup and pop into a frying pan, gills up, with enough nicely browned garlic oil (enough is an $\frac{1}{8}$ in/3 mm layer in a close-fitting pan) and put on a lid. Heat over a moderate flame until the mushrooms are really slack, and the white tops have browned a bit. Add a splash of soya sauce or salt to taste, a chicken stock cube or two from the freezer, pepper to taste, a squeeze of lemon or a splash of dry white wine, and enough fresh-chopped herb to look good.

I've talked about interchanging herbs with flippancy but adding a smoky fresh herb does

turn the flavour of cultivated mushrooms into one reminiscent of wild mushrooms, and I have to confess that fresh thyme does this transformation better than any other. For a real wild mushroom taste, add a few soaked, dried ceps with their juice before frying. Fresh ceps are terrific cooked this way.

Serve them in their near black sauce and separated oil. Or emulsify the sauce with thick cream; it masks the flavour but the dish can stand that. Keep some of the fresh herb to sprinkle on top. This dish is an excellent light starter or a nice savoury snack with some crisp-fried bacon on well-buttered toast.

Hot beetroot starter

Makes 1 portion
4–5 oz (115–140 g) young beetroot
1 oz (30 g) salted butter
1 tablespoon lemon juice
salt and pepper to taste

Boil unpeeled beets until soft in salted water. Allow to cool; peel and slice them about $\frac{1}{8}$ in (3 mm) thick. These slices are layered in individual ramekins with thin slices of butter, a generous amount of fresh ground pepper, a good squeeze of lemon and a pinch of salt on each layer (a butter vinaigrette of sorts). Finish with dabs of butter.

This dish can be prepared ahead up to this point. Skin them with clingfilm, to retard the drying of the top layer, and they will keep for a couple of days in the fridge.

Heat them in a medium oven for half an hour, replacing the clingfilm with aluminium foil. On the other hand, the micro is splendid for warming these up – keep the clingfilm in this case.

Savoury green salad

This dish was inspired by salmagundy, an old-fashioned salad of salty, piquant, sweet, crisp and creamy ingredients. It included some or all of the following: pickled fish, cold roast meats, cheese, fried croutons, a variety of cooked and raw vegetables, salad greens and herbs. Such a salad would hardly need anything other than a pudding to round it off.

This salad is a much lighter affair but not light enough to be thought of as a side dish to a main course nor as a palate cleanser after one. Think of it as a mixture of salad and main course.

Serves 4

Main course
6 oz (170 g) rump steak
6–8 oz (170–225 g) baby new potatoes
3 oz (85 g) slim green beans
1 large clove garlic
2 teaspoons lemon juice
2 teaspoons soy sauce
½ teaspoon sugar
½ in (1.25 cm) chilli
½ teaspoon dried thyme
1 dessertspoon cooking oil

Salad
1 frisée, or curly endive
1 handful young spinach leaves
4 spring onions (or the equivalent in sweet, white or red, skinned onions)
2 stalks of celery
1 tablespoon fresh herb leaves
vinaigrette

Cut the steak into ½ in (1.25 cm) slices, across the grain, then cut these into ½ in (1.25 cm) matchsticks. Put these into a marinade made of lemon juice, soy, sugar, chilli and thyme for no more than two hours. Clean and boil the potatoes and let them cool; top and tail the beans and blanch them in salted boiling water for two minutes and rinse cold.

Prepare the salad using the white and yellow part of the frisée; trim the stalks from the spinach; trim and split the spring onions into four, lengthwise, and put into iced water to curl; trim and diagonally slice the celery; strip the leaves from the stalks of the herbs; make the vinaigrette (see p. 132).

Heat the oil, smoking hot, in a frying pan; crush or sliver the garlic and put into the pan with the meat. Sear the strips, stirring occasionally, until parts of them are brown (about two minutes – the idea is to sear and crisp but leave the strips pink inside); remove from the pan to a warm place. Cool the pan a little and pour in the marinade to reduce. At the last minute, roll the meat and juices in the marinade. Reheat potatoes (cut into bite-sized pieces) and the beans, either in a microwave or in boiling water. Assemble all the ingredients and toss in vinaigrette.

Variations

Feta Use Feta cheese instead of the meat and cooked vegetables.

4 oz (115 g) Feta cheese
1 level teaspoon each of paprika, dried thyme
*   and bright (or freshly grated black) pepper*
1 tablespoon garlic oil

Put the cheese into a frying pan and dress the top with half of the paprika, pepper, thyme and oil. Grill this until the thyme has charred a little. Let this cool then turn it over and do the same to the other side. When it is completely cold, cut the cheese into cubes and put into the salad with the oil.

Croutons For a lighter salad use croutons.

2 or 3 slices of bread
garlic oil to taste
a sprinkle of dried thyme and pepper

Lightly toast each slice then brush each side with garlic oil, thyme and pepper and re-toast until nicely brown. Cut into cubes and keep dry and warm.

This salad is tailored to fit in with the menu on p. 151 but the permutations are endless. Think of this example as a combination of sensations and match the ingredients. Here, I've ignored the potential of fruit, nuts, pickled or canned fish and much more.

Roast vegetables

Potatoes

Peel the potatoes and cut into suitable sized pieces. Sometimes I leave the skin on for the extra flavour it adds, but in this recipe I peel them because a crust forms better on peeled surfaces. Raw potatoes tend to dry out with a hard crust if they are roasted long enough to cook soft inside. Avoid this drying out by par-cooking them first. The microwave makes this

effortless, but par-boiling peeled potatoes in salted water will be fine. Allow from a third to a half of the full cooking time; leave them in the cooking water until cool enough to handle and then score runnels over their surfaces with a fork. Put them into a shallow baking tray, coat with melted butter or garlic oil (the runnels will hold this oil and help with the browning) and place into a hot oven (220°C/425°F/Gas Mark 7) for 30 minutes. Turn the potatoes, so that they brown on all sides, and baste them from time to time. A fine sprinkle of salt before roasting makes them irresistible, hot or cold.

Parsnips, carrots, celeriac and yams

All these are suitable for similar treatment.

Small onions

Peeling raw onions is a drag; small ones are even worse. Boil small ones in their skins and peel them when they are cool – it is so much easier. Roast as above but without the scored surfaces. They are delicious roasted around a joint, but if you are roasting them separately, an interesting variation is to be had by introducing a little vinegar, sugar and salt into the basting juices. The Italians call this *cipolline in agrodulce* (baby onions in sweet-sour sauce).

Baked onions

Spanish onions, the size of a fist, are lovely baked in their skins. It takes about an hour (or less if a microwave is used) for the flesh to soften and for the juices to run out of the top and brown with a delicious Maillard effect. Cut them in half with a very sharp knife and serve with butter, salt and a sprinkle of vinegar. A wise old lady I admire swears that these onions give the deepest, sweetest sleep of all.

Charred red peppers

There is a way of serving red peppers where they are skinned before being dressed with good olive oil and served as a starter. Skinning starts with burning the pepper, over a flame, until the skin has blackened and blistered; the pepper is then popped into a bag for the heat and steam to slacken the skin still sticking to the flesh. Burning the skin in this way intensifies the flavour of the pepper and, although the skin has been completely removed when served, it makes this dish infinitely more compulsive than the same dish where the skin has been removed with steam or par-boiling.

There is an easier way of getting this intensity. Split a pepper down the middle and remove stalk and seeds from both halves. Cut each half into $\frac{1}{4}$ in (6 mm) thin strips. Lay these skin side up, like some exotic carpet, in a frying pan, breaking the flesh underneath, or trimming protuberances where necessary to get the flatness needed for even grilling. Grill until the skin is nicely and evenly browned. Since the skin is in pieces small enough for the mouth to handle easily, there is no need for it to be removed. Dress with a fragrant lemon juice and garlic oil vinaigrette. I like them served with shreds of anchovies too.

Fried potato segments

From this recipe you get a pan-fried potato segment, the taste of which is that of baked potato skin and browned garlic. Bits of garlic fry onto the open sides of the segment and look very pretty. It will have a floury inside, just like a well-baked potato, and a fried crunchy edge where the segment is thinnest, away from the skin. Bliss!

Take a baking potato, one that becomes floury inside when cooked, and microwave until it is well heated inside but not too soft; about 4–5 minutes (par-boiling the potato for between a third and a half of the usual boiling time and leaving the potato in the hot water is almost as good). If possible, leave the whole potato time to cool before cutting, it is less delicate then. Cut it in half and place each side cut face down before cutting into segments. This way the skin stays firmly on the flesh. Cut three segments from each half, or two from a small half. Heat some garlic oil in a pan and, before it gets brown, introduce the potatoes. First brown one face of each segment and then the other and, if you're enthusiastic about the taste of well-browned, baked potato skin, the skin side too. That is all there is to it.

Sauces

Béchamel sauce

This is a thick bland white sauce used as a vehicle to carry other flavours both sweet and savoury and to thicken a sauce that is too liquid.

Wheat flour thickens ten times its weight of liquid and this easily remembered ratio makes the recipe for béchamel simple to write. To one part each of butter and flour add ten parts of hot milk or cream.

Melt the butter in a saucepan, add the flour and stir, over heat, until they are combined and smooth. This butter/flour liaison is known as a roux. Add the liquid a little at a time, stirring in thoroughly before adding more. There is one critical moment in making béchamel when the sauce becomes so liquid that any lumps left in it are able to flow away from the spoon that is stirring the sauce. Straining these lumps out is tedious so watch for the moment when the stirring spoon hardly reveals the bottom of the saucepan anymore and, at that point, do a thorough job of beating out the lumps for good. Add hot but not boiling liquid and make a faster job of it. The sauce continues to thicken until it boils.

Change the ratio to one part flour to seven parts liquid to make a thicker sauce suitable for making béchamel cubes for the freezer (see p. 163).

For extra flavour and a brown sauce, heat the roux until the flour is brown before adding liquid. This sauce is one used for meat stews and is also the basis for an infamous soup called Brown Windsor, which has haunted the reputation of British cooking since Victorian times.

Duxelles

This is the name given to a purée of sweated shallots and white mushrooms. Use duxelles as a wonderfully enriching, mushroomy flavour base for sauces and soups. Added to a plain white béchamel sauce (see above), it makes a satisfying sauce to mix with cooked vegetables. With added cheese, this is the sauce for such homely but delicious dishes as cauliflower cheese. I prefer the flavour of duxelles when the shallots have been browned and the mushrooms are dark and flavourful, it may look like sludge and muddy the colour of the sauce, but sometimes the gain in flavour is worth the loss of whiteness or clear bright colour.

1 lb (450 g) finely chopped mushrooms
4 oz (115 g) salted butter
2 fl oz (55 ml) sunflower or peanut oil
2 oz (55 g) shallots, finely chopped
salt, pepper and ground mace to taste
MSG (a good pinch, if you can stand the thought)
1 eggcupful fine chopped parsley, tarragon or
    other sweet herb

Melt the butter and oil together and heat until the butter curds begin to turn brown. Add the mushrooms, shallots and seasoning and cook

slowly, stirring occasionally, until the mushrooms are soft. Let the mixture cool, then keep it, in a screw-topped jar, in the fridge for a week or freeze. Add the fresh herb just before use.

Hollandaise Sauce

This warm, buttery sauce is made as you would make mayonnaise but using melted butter instead of oil. Extra thickness is to be had by warming up the sauce gently until the eggs in it begin to thicken noticeably. Methods of making it are legion, but, if you have the nerve for it, the speedy way we used at the restaurant was to mix the flavoured vinegar with egg yolks, just like any other method, and, using a hand-held blender, beat in hot melted butter from the microwave. The heat of the butter cooks the yolks to the required thickness. For home use I can't recommend this way unless you live for hollandaise – when the speed of making would make it worthwhile to master. It is a good deal safer to make it more slowly, ahead of time, and keep it warm.

3 tablespoons vinegar
1 large shallot
3–4 egg yolks
6 oz (170 g) butter

Make a shallot vinegar by slicing, as thin as you can, one largish shallot and covering it with 3 tablespoons of white wine vinegar, a heavy pinch of salt and a light pinch of sugar.

Leave it marinating for 30 minutes (or 20 seconds in the microwave) and strain. Don't throw away the pickled shallots – they are superb in salads or sandwiches.

Add to this vinegar a tablespoon of water and 3–4 egg yolks. Beating all the time with a whisk or using a processor or a hand-held blender, add the warm melted butter (to get a thicker sauce, use clarified butter, see pp. 59–60). Heat up this liaison, oh so gently, in a double boiler or a basin fitting tightly on a small pan of boiling water so that it traps most of the steam. Stir continually until the sauce thickens to a pouring custard thickness. Remove from the heat and – lest it curdles – pour the sauce into another, cooler basin, but keep lukewarm. Clingfilm the top if it is to be kept waiting, as it skins easily. If it does separate, add water, beating furiously while you do it. Some start with a dessertspoon of water and beat the separated sauce into it gradually just as if they were starting from scratch.

Stir in a good handful of well-chopped tarragon leaves, and hollandaise becomes béarnaise. I add a touch of mustard too. This a splendid sauce with barbecued fish or steak and well-fried pommes frites.

Vinaigrette

1 level teaspoon sea salt
½ level teaspoon sugar
½ level teaspoon fresh ground pepper
½ level teaspoon mustard powder
1 tablespoon wine vinegar
4 tablespoons good olive oil
1 tablespoon garlic oil

Mix all the ingredients together and pour into a screw-topped jar. Give this jar a really good shake before each use. Vinaigrette can be made to thicken rather like mayonnaise – just add the oil, drop by drop, to a mixture of the other ingredients, beating or blending all the time. The liaison thus formed is delicate and quite often separates, but given a shake some measure of blending returns.

This is a straightforward vinaigrette suitable for green salads. The combined sense appeal of all the ingredients in it is so good that it is put to use in many other sauces. For example – mayonnaise is vinaigrette with egg, hollandaise is mayonnaise with butter not oil, maltaise is mayonnaise with orange juice not lemon, etc. Since all the ingredients can be changed without lessening its sense appeal the variety is endless.

Variations for green salads

Lemon juice can be used for vinegar; honey for sugar; ready-made mustard (French, German, whole-grain, etc.) for mustard powder; bright pepper for black peppercorn pepper (see p. 167); walnut oil, etc. for olive oil. Change the proportions according to the strength of the substitute.

Variations for other salads

For salads with stronger ingredients, warm piquant salads or where a salad becomes more of a course in its own right – like salmagundy – the range of variants is even wider. Something else salty could replace the sea salt – olive purée, mashed anchovies or soy sauce perhaps. Sweet fruit purée, dried or fresh can replace sugar or honey; fresh or dried chilli instead of pepper; and horseradish instead of mustard. Sharp fruit like tamarind, which is sweet as well as sharp, substitutes well for both vinegar and sugar.

Heat the garlic oil until the morsels of garlic are light brown before assembling to make browned garlic vinaigrette, which is a good dressing for hot vegetables.

The only restriction on the choice is that the substitute used provides the taste or mouth texture stimulus of the original. Keep an eye on sauce recipes; it is surprising how often the vinaigrette formula crops up in them.

Satay sauce

There are as many ways of making this sauce as there are cooks who make it. My version takes advantage of peanut butter, off the shelf, instead of the more traditional roasting and grinding of peanuts. Serve it with small skewers of lamb, with beef kebab, with any grilled marinated meats or with soft egg noodles as part of a variety of dishes with a Far Eastern bias.

1 tablespoon garlic oil
1 fresh chilli pepper
1 mustardspoon balachan (see p. 81)
1 tablespoon peanut butter
1 tablespoon hoisin sauce
1 lime – both zest and juice
1 in (3 cm) fresh ginger root
1 large shallot
1 tablespoon soy sauce

Fry the chilli, finely chopped, in garlic oil until the chilli pieces are reduced in size and beginning to brown. Add the balachan – I've only allowed for a mild sauce, but if pungency is needed to balance a strong-flavoured meat, then increasing the amount by up to three times won't be overstrong. Add the peanut butter – take the pan off the heat before adding to allow the butter to slacken and blend with the oil without burning. Add lime juice and zest and hoisin sauce.

Bring to the boil with 2 tablespoons water and allow to thicken. If the sauce separates, add more water and boil again.

Add finely chopped ginger and shallot, bring to the boil for a brief second or two, taste and add the soy sauce – I've said a tablespoonful but that could be too much or not enough, depending on personal preference.

Prawn sambal

This is a fishy, chilli hot and rich sauce, served separately to the course for which it is intended. It is given here as an admirable complement to the Malayan fish soup Laksa but is splendid with noodles too.

1 teaspoon balachan (see p. 81), grated
½ small red chilli
¼ pint (140 ml) of garlic oil
1 tablespoon small prawns
1 teaspoon hot paprika
1 teaspoon tomato purée

Fry the grated balachan in garlic oil with the chilli for a few minutes until the garlic, in the oil, is brown. Add some small peeled prawns and fry them until they are reduced in size and chewy; then colour the oily mixture with paprika and concentrated tomato purée. There should be enough oil to make it a pourable sauce. I like a squeeze or two of lime in this sauce too.

As for the chilli, the size I'm thinking of is anything from two to six inches (5–15 cm) but the heat of it is rather more important than its size. The heat in a chilli is most pronounced in the white pulpy fibre that attaches the seeds to the skin.

Relishes

In Chapter 4 on what should be done to food after cooking, I make great play with the idea that cooked food, wonderful and rich though it may be, can always be made more attention-grabbing if the dish has something fresh served with or in it. Relishes – think of them as short-life pickles – fit this bill very nicely, being quick to make and deliciously fresh. They should be served as a side dish, as this allows them to be passed around the table, not when the dish is served but after a mouthful or two. In this way the dish is given a chance of being tasted with and without the relish; obviously a good idea in terms of attracting attention and therefore increasing the pleasure of eating the dish.

Freshly made relishes have more or less the same ingredients as bottled pickles but, since they are intended for consumption immediately and are not to be kept on the kitchen shelf for months, the preserving elements – salt, sugar and vinegar – can be applied with a lighter hand allowing the fresh elements to retain some character.

Any of the vegetables that are normally thought suitable candidates for pickling (i.e. garlic, onions, cucumbers and courgettes, fresh chillies, capsicums, red cabbage, tomatoes and cauliflower) can be used in a relish with the addition of fresh herbs, in quantity, to give them an extra dimension.

The basic method is to put enough salt in some vinegar for it to bite the tongue (roughly ¼ oz/7 g salt to 1 oz/30 ml of vinegar); if the vegetable to be pickled has some bitterness (like cabbage or cucumber), add a similar amount of sugar. Slice the vegetables thinly or chop into small dice and submerge in the pickle. The smaller the pieces, or the thinner the slicing, the faster the pickling. The acid in the dressing works faster than usual because of the generous amount of salt present, which accelerates the exchange of vegetable juices with the acids. Ten minutes is enough to take the sting out of thinly sliced onions and twenty will make fine-chopped fresh chilli approachable. Serve them drained of the vinegar.

I particularly like what this technique does to the flavour of cucumber, probably because I grew up with cucumber salad – in effect a relish where thinly sliced cucumber is allowed to soften in salted and sugared vinegar – served with cold poached salmon. Any left-over salad was made into a now-forgotten tea table delicacy of crustless, thickly buttered, cucumber sandwiches.

The amount of salt needed to produce instant pickle makes the pickling vinegar too strong to serve with the relish. But it would be a shame to throw it away. It can be used as the salt and vinegar part of vinaigrette or mayonnaise. Don't use it if cabbage or cauliflower

have been paddling in it – the raw juices from these are not pleasant – but when onions, chilli, cucumber or tomatoes have left their juices behind, it is quite another matter.

Cucumber and fresh green chilli relish

This example uses the basic-method, instant-pickle formula given above as a canvas and shows how it might be embroidered on.

Salt 4 oz (115 ml) of white wine vinegar until it pricks the tongue and sweeten it with a teaspoon of sugar. Add 1 tablespoon of garlic oil, 1 teaspoon of fine chopped green or red fresh chilli and 1 thinly sliced garlic clove.

After 10 minutes, add 3 tablespoons of cucumber cut into $\frac{1}{4}$ in (6 mm) cubes, skin and all. In another 10 minutes, when the pickle has taken the sting out of these, strain (but keep the juice as a basis for an interesting vinaigrette) and add 2 tablespoons of chopped herb – parsley will do nicely but mint or basil is great. If this relish packs too much punch, add some fresh-chopped tomatoes which will dilute the flavour and make it look more interesting. Notice how the densest material has the longest marinade – the frailest almost nothing at all.

Pickled shallot relish for a salad

Make the basic-method relish of sweetened salty vinegar (as above) and pop a very thinly sliced shallot into it for five minutes. Strain and put the slightly softened shallots into the salad and the salty vinegar into the vinaigrette.

Red cabbage relish

To a good handful of *very thinly cut* red cabbage add a teaspoon or two of salt and about half that amount of sugar. After half an hour (or, if the slicing has been really fine, as little as fifteen minutes) add a dessertspoon of vinegar and the same of fine-chopped onions. Almost by the time it gets to the table it will be ready to eat. Exactly the same recipe is used for red cabbage pickle, which will last for months as long as the cabbage is completely covered by the vinegar.

However, it won't have the crunch that this instant relish has. I usually serve this relish with cold cuts, since I grew up having it with cold roast lamb on a Monday, after hot roast lamb on Sunday but before, of course, the lamb stew on Tuesday and the minced lamb and potato rissoles on Wednesday (this was the old Yorkshire way of stretching meat to last through the week and is so ingrained in my mind as to have a regular, almost playground skipping chant to it).

Mushroom relish

You would hardly recognize this relish if you are used to the commercial variety, which is much less mushroomy. The first time I tasted it, the relish had been made from an extra large haul of field mushrooms, and this was a way of using those fly-blown oddments not suitable for drying.

Put an inch (25 mm) layer of mushroom refuse – that is the stalks, peelings and other wizened mushroom bits – in a preserving jar and sprinkle on $\frac{3}{8}$ in (10 mm) of salt. Keep topping up the jar with mushrooms and salt as they come to hand – we make this relish in September, when there is usually quite a lot. Put a weight – I use a flat pebble – on top of the mushrooms to ensure that the juices from them cover the surface. This stops mould growing on the top layer. Within a fortnight or so the salt will have drawn the juice from the refuse. Strain off the solids and you have mushroom relish. It will keep well if kept cold.

What I have given here is the basic recipe but this is improved by adding a pinch of sugar and MSG powder with each salt layer and introducing a few cloves of garlic, here and there, through the layers.

Use mushroom relish instead of soy sauce in Chinese dishes or with steaks or poached fish, but it really comes into its own served with bacon and eggs.

Pesto

This Italian sauce of fresh basil, ground with fresh garlic, pine kernels, Parmesan and fruity olive oil, shows how effective the relish technique can be. It can be bought ready-made in jars, but the colour of it through the glass jar tells it all. That flat grey/green has nothing of the excitement of the dark emerald basil that colours the freshly made sauce, and the taste is equally disappointing. Freshly made pesto will transform the dreariest soup and the plainest pasta into absolute glory, and the fresher the making, the greater the glory.

To a large bunch of basil – a good open handful – add a clove of garlic or two, 1 oz (30 g) each of freshly grated Parmesan and pine kernels (lightly toasted for an extra bite). Grind the lot together in a processor, or traditionally with a pestle and mortar, with enough olive oil to make a dark green purée, add salt to taste and that is all there is to it. *Miracolo* – but only for a brief half hour or so and then the brilliant green turns muddy.

This relish is so good because the basil works aromatic magic on top of what seems to be a very sound formula for arousing the senses. All the ingredients used can be changed, with discretion, and still the formula works. Here are a few changes/replacements that I've made with some success, and the thinking that lies behind them.

Changing the ingredients

Herbs Use fresh green herb as a substitute for basil. Its nearest relative, mint, gets closer to the original flavour than any other. The more aromatic the herb, the better the relish. Two herbs can be combined to increase the depth of flavour, but if the grinding is too fine they lose their identity; chop them instead of grinding them, and there is a chance that both tastes can be enjoyed separately. Mint and fennel is a good combination as is the anise-flavoured tarragon with the aromatic, celery-flavoured lovage.

Garlic Replace garlic with shallots or spring onions. Both of these are weaker than garlic, so use more of them. Remember, do, that onions deteriorate quickly once cut, so don't make this relish before you need it.

Parmesan This cheese gains strength from being aged and dried out, with its taste-diluting liquid evaporated. Any really mature cheese – Pecorino, Sardo or very old Gouda for instance – will approximate Parmesan's intensity for this sauce.

Pine kernels Called *pinoli* in Italy, these are the mildest of nuts and most others will add more flavour to the relish, so fewer will be needed. Most of the nuts that spring to mind as substitutes have bitter skins, which will need removing if the relish is to retain its green fresh character.

Olive oil There is no other oil that has as pronounced a flavour, so substitution will certainly lessen the relish's impact but if the nuts being used can be complemented by the same nut oil – peanuts with peanut oil, hazelnuts with hazelnut oil, etc. – the combined taste will go some way in compensation. Resist the temptation to use toasted nut oils, they have such a strong taste that the quantity needed will swamp the relish.

Gremolata

This relish is a way of adding freshness and cutting the richness of stews, which is worth bearing in mind when contemplating making such dishes as ox-tail. The Italians add it to a bony veal stew called *osso buco*. It is nothing more than a handful of chopped fresh herb (parsley is the usual one), mixed with a finely chopped clove of garlic and the zest of half a lemon, which is added to a stew immediately before serving. As is obvious, this is a relish without acidity and it opens a new avenue to explore since most other relishes contain at least a modicum of it. Keeping fresh herbs back to add after cooking is sound attention-seeking

practice anyway, and this way of doing it is brilliant.

Chutneys

It wouldn't seem right to leave this section without giving two chutney recipes just to show how low-profile most ready-made Western chutneys are. The first is a simple Middle Eastern lemon chutney – simple and quick and very bright, almost a relish. The second is the first Indian chutney I ever made. It bowled me over with its complexity in the fifties and still does now with much more experience of eating Indian food behind me. Give it a whirl, just once, to know how far palate massage can go.

Lemon chutney

Cut up a whole lemon into $\frac{1}{8}$ in (3 mm) slices and the slices into segments, each with its own piece of rind. Spread these on a plate and freeze solid; it doesn't take too long. The freezing expands the liquid in the rind, making it soft and receptive. Remove them from the freezer and sprinkle with a teaspoon or two of salt, then wait until they are soft – about an hour. Immerse in mild olive oil, coloured a rich red-orange with paprika. That's it.

A deeper taste can be had by freezing fine slices of garlic in with the lemon. To gild the lily use a pinch of bright pepper (see p. 167). This is brilliant with grilled meats and even makes plain boiled rice interesting. Before I discovered how rapidly the lemon segments soften with freezing, this chutney took a month to ripen. Change the flavour by using Seville oranges (which is nice with a fatty roast duck) or limes (with grilled herrings).

Sharp fruit chutney

12 oz (340 g) Bramley apples
12 oz (340 g) plums
1 lb (450 g) brown sugar
8 fl oz (225 ml) vinegar
2 tablespoons of sultanas, currants or raisins
2 whole heads garlic, peeled and chopped
2 teaspoons garam masala (see pp. 167–8)
1 teaspoon caraway
1 or 2 teaspoons chilli powder (or the equivalent in chopped fresh chilli – roughly 3 times the bulk of the powder)
1–2 in (2.5–5 cm) fresh ginger, cut fine
$\frac{3}{4}$ oz (20 g) salt

Stone the plums and core the apples. Cut the fruit up so that the skin is in $\frac{1}{4}$ in (6 mm) bits to make it easier to manage on the plate. Bring all the ingredients to the boil in a stainless steel or enamelled pan, then simmer for 30–40 minutes, with an occasional stir to stop it catching; cool and bottle. This pickle improves with keeping.

Seasoned Butters

These are really uncooked sauces waiting to be melted onto hot dishes. Their value lies in being ready-made and available at any time directly from the freezer.

Roll the flavoured butter into a $1\frac{1}{2}$ in (4 cm) diameter sausage then cut into $\frac{1}{4}$ in (7 mm) medallions. Layer them, not touching, and freeze. Once hard, they can be bagged and still be available, one at a time, as needed.

Maître d'hôtel butter

Here fine-chopped fresh herbs, lemon juice and zest, pepper and salt are mixed with softened butter – in other words, a sort of herb vinaigrette made with butter not oil. Traditionally this is used, thawed, on steak or any other grilled meat or fish (the herbs used in the butter for white fish should be sweet rather than smoky).

Garlic butter

This is as above but with garlic oil added. The addition of oil makes the butter very soft, so get the mixture good and cold before trying to shape it. Use as you would *maître d'hôtel* butter, but more sparingly. This is the version to use for garlic bread and is good with grilled mushrooms too.

Anchovy butter

Again, this is *maître d'hôtel* butter but with fine-chopped anchovies, or good quality anchovy paste, and capers. Use meltingly, with boiled meats, fish or potatoes.

Suzette butter

Mix orange zest and sugar with salted butter. This is excellent in place of the more usual Suzette sauce. Splash a drop or three of orange liqueur onto a pudding (or hot cake) before placing the medallion in place for the brilliant alcohol/sugar/butter effect to work its magic.

Savoury Oddments

Salted almonds

Pour boiling water onto whole almonds to loosen their skins. Take them out of the water, a few at a time, and squeeze them so that the skin rotates and the kernel point breaks through it; most of the almonds will pop out of their skins easily. Almonds absorb water and their white flesh soon becomes semi-transparent. This spoils their frying quality so skin at speed with tingling fingertips or, if the damage has been done, split them and leave to dry out in a warm place for a day.

I don't know an easy way to split almonds, but I do it with a sharp knife, the point of which I insert into the indentation in the nut where the two halves join. Halving them while they are warm makes it a bit easier. Why split them at all? Fried almonds are crunchy and, if they are split, there will be twice as much crunch and biting into them is easier.

Frying nuts is tricky; once they start to brown, they do it fast. Put them in hot oil and stir continuously while they first blanch and then start to brown. Remove them from the oil immediately onto absorbent paper, where they will continue to brown in their own heat. This browning is very easily overdone. I like them a lighter brown than commercially roasted nuts since they look home-made and taste more like almonds. Keep them in an airtight tin and use them to give crunch to soft-textured dishes or, salted, with drinks. Make them more unusual by grinding sea salt with toasted cumin and caraway seeds and powder the still-hot nuts with this mixture to raise an eyebrow or two. Better yet, flavour some with cumin salt and others with caraway salt, so that, although the almonds will look alike, some will taste different. Little surprises like this make food taste better because eaters of it think, if only for a second, about what they are eating.

Pan-fried and grilled bread

1 oz (30 g) yeast
2 tablespoons milk (with 2 teaspoons sugar)
1 lb (450 g) strong flour
2 teaspoons salt
1 tablespoon olive oil
12 oz (340 ml) warm water (approx.)
1 teaspoon mixed dried herbs

1 tablespoon garlic oil (p. 165), browned

4 dried tomatoes, chopped

2 tablespoons grated strong cheese (Parmesan type)

zest of $\frac{1}{2}$ lemon, grated

Foam the yeast in a little warm, sweetened milk, add it to the strong flour, salt and olive oil and add enough of the warm water to make a slack dough.

Let it rise in a warm, covered place until twice its original bulk, add the rest of the ingredients, mix into the dough and spread it $\frac{1}{2}$ in (12 mm) thick onto an oiled, shallow baking tray to rise again. Sprinkle the top with more cheese and bake for 15 minutes in a hot oven (220°C/425°F/Gas Mark 7) until nicely brown on top.

Alternatively, let it take its second rise in a well-oiled frying pan. When nicely risen, put the pan on a low heat until a firm bottom crust has formed in the pan, then place it under a low medium grill until it looks right, nicely brown and hollow sounding to a finger tap. Eat hot with antipasti or with creamy yoghurt as a canapé.

Fresh breadcrumb-stuffing balls

Putting a flavoured stuffing into the cavity of a bird (or a hole in a joint of meat where the bone has been removed) adds flavour to the flesh and keeps it moist. That is the conventional wisdom, but I find that the flavour it adds to the flesh is marginal compared to the

flavour of the stuffing eaten at the same time. And, since it is wrapped around by flesh, by the time enough heat has penetrated for the stuffing to be cooked the flesh must be overcooked – hardly keeping it moist.

I'm all in favour of having the taste of stuffing on the plate, but it can be cooked in the baking pan, where it will benefit from the juices while it is cooking and be browned too.

10 oz (285 g) fresh breadcrumbs

5 oz (140 g) fine chopped onion

3 oz (85 g) butter or fat trimmed from the joint before roasting

2–3 oz (55–85 g) of grated juicy flavour (celery, carrot or apple)

1$\frac{1}{2}$ oz (45 g) fresh herb

2 heaped teaspoons dried herb

zest and juice of $\frac{1}{2}$ lemon

chilli to taste (start with $\frac{1}{2}$ teaspoon of fine-chopped, fresh chilli or 1 teaspoon of chilli oil or vinegar)

Mix all ingredients together, roll into balls and, a good 20–30 minutes before serving – longer if the oven is cool or the baking tray is deep – drop them into the baking pan containing the roast, rolling them around in the juices. Better still, pour off the juices into a separate shallow tray and bake the stuffing balls in that – they will get browner that way.

Pork crackling

Tough pork skin expands during cooking and makes a crunchy coating called crackling. Thick pork skin crackles best.

It helps a lot if the rind is scored, or cut deep, well into the underlying fat, and the cuts are $\frac{1}{4}$ in (6 mm) apart. The roasting skin starts to bubble on these cut edges first, so the more cuts the better. Rub the skin with garlic oil, then salt, before roasting to get a better crackle. Get the oven really hot before putting the joint in and aim to get the skin well on its way to crackling before lowering the temperature. Baste the skin frequently with hot fat from the baking pan for, if the fat is hot enough, it will cause the skin to bubble a little as it is being poured on. If there is still trouble in getting the crunch, cut off the skin and high-roast it separately in a shallow pan. But while separate cooking pretty well guarantees crunchy blisters all the way through, it cooks the underlying fat a crisp brown too, which is a pity since the succulence of translucent fat is part of pork crackling's charm.

Garlic croutons

Take slices of pre-sliced frozen bread from the freezer and paint both sides with garlic oil. Toast for a fraction longer than usual to allow the surface to brown as the interior defrosts.

I'm no advocate of sliced bread but it has worked its way into my life because it keeps so well in the freezer. It is available there, a slice at a time, without the lengthy defrost of a whole loaf. In this recipe frozen bread is not only convenient, it makes a better crouton. Paint oil onto unfrozen bread and it soaks it up like blotting paper; when it is frozen it won't, also less oil is used and what is used is more evenly spread. The frozen interior gives time for the surface of a slice, with its garlic oil coating, to get thoroughly brown while the inside stays moist.

Puddings

Alexander pudding

Makes 6 small ramekins
4 oz (115 g) butter
4 oz (115 g) sugar
3 eggs
6 oz (170 g) fresh breadcrumbs
1 tablespoon frozen orange rind or marmalade,
   fine chopped
1 lemon
orange liqueur

Cream the sugar and butter in a bowl and blend in the 3 egg yolks. Add the juice and zest of the lemon and the chopped orange. Stir in the fresh breadcrumbs, then add 3 whipped egg whites. Pour the mixture into well-buttered 3 in (8 cm) ramekins up to three-quarters full. Steam for half an hour, or until a skewer pushed into the centre of a pudding comes out clean. Turn out the puddings and pour on each 1 teaspoon of orange liqueur. Serve with rich egg custard.

I use a zester to get the zest from the lemon. It comes off in tiny curls which retain most of their oil; use a grater and you can see this oil being lost. Frozen citrus peel softens as it thaws so that it seems almost pre-cooked but it keeps a zingy freshness not to be found in marmalade – a softer, sweeter alternative. Any sort of orange liqueur will do to dress the puddings, but use, if you can find it, Aurum, an Italian bergamot orange liqueur with a strong, aromatic, orange zest nose. Look for it in the best Italian shops or scour the back streets of Siena. In Italy it has a low, old-hat image, but it is quite wonderful.

If you haven't a steamer take a large, lidded, saucepan and prop up a plate in it so that it rests securely about a third of the way up from the bottom. As a support for this, use a suitably sized basin with enough water in it to make it stable. Pour 1 in (2.5 cm) of boiling water into the pan, place the ramekins on the plate and cover them with buttered paper before putting the lid on. The butter will stop the puddings sticking to the paper and the paper protects them from condensation. These individual puddings freeze very well.

Rich egg custard

½ pt (285 ml) cream (or milk with a walnut of
*   butter)*
2 oz (55 g) sugar or honey (2 tablespoons)
4 egg yolks or 2 whole eggs
1 vanilla pod
lemon zest

Simmer the milk with the sugar or honey, a vanilla pod, a thumbnail or two of lemon zest and a walnut of butter for 10–15 minutes. You can use cream instead of milk and butter.

Beat 4 egg yolks (or 2 yolks and whites) in a large enough basin to take the total mix and pour in the sieved milk.

Put the basin into a pan just big enough to take it with 2 in (5 cm) of water in the bottom. Heat the pan and stir the mixture gently, but thoroughly, until it is thick enough to coat the back of the spoon. This is a ticklish moment: too much heat and the mix will continue to heat and curdle, not enough and the custard will be too thin to satisfy. Watch carefully and you will notice a moment when it stops being a thin cream and begins to show a thicker covering of the spoon. Remove immediately and pour into the serving bowl. The cool bowl will take heat from the custard and put it out of danger of curdling.

Cover the surface of the custard with clingfilm to stop a skin forming and keep in a warm place until needed. Thin with cream if necessary.

Little pot of chocolate

Makes 5 or more ramekins
4 oz (115 g) plain chocolate
½ oz (15 g) unsweetened cocoa powder
1 teaspoon best instant-coffee powder
2 tablespoons alcohol
3 oz (85 g) butter
2 egg yolks
3 egg whites
2 oz (55 g) caster sugar

Melt the chocolate and add the softened butter, cocoa, coffee powder and alcohol. Stir in the egg yolks, one at a time, which should be at room temperature.

Whisk the whites to whiteness and beat in the sugar until the 'soft peak' stage. Add a quarter of the chocolate mix to the whites and stir in gently but thoroughly. Add the rest of the chocolate mixture, mixing gently, more folding in than stirring. Pour into ramekins, cover with clingfilm (don't let it touch the surface of the mousse) to inhibit a crust, and chill.

This amount will fill $5\frac{1}{2}$ ramekins ($3\frac{1}{2}$ in/9 cm in diameter by $1\frac{1}{2}$ in/4 cm deep), 6 if you're careful. Parsimony can be a blessing at times and here is one of those times, for this pot is rich indeed.

The chocolate should be best quality with minimum butterfat. I use Chocolat Menier (47 per cent cocoa) and Van Houten cocoa powder. The alcohol I prefer is brandy, but rum or a fruit liqueur is fine.

Amber's chocolate orange mousse

This mousse is lighter than the chocolate pot above and zingy with the zest. Quite delicious, thank you Amber.

Makes 7 ramekins ($3\frac{1}{2} \times 1\frac{1}{2}$ in/9 × 4 cm)
7 oz (200 g) best dark chocolate
4 egg yolks
5 egg whites
zest of ½ orange

Melt the chocolate with a squeeze of orange juice, stir in the yolks and curls of zest. Beat the whites to soft peaks and stir in bit by bit. Pour into the ramekins, or into a serving bowl, and cover the top with grated chocolate. Mature in the fridge for a day.

Crème brûlée

Makes 6 or more ramekins ($3\frac{1}{2} \times 1\frac{1}{2}$ in/9 × 4 cm)
1 pint (570 ml) cream or milk enriched with ½ oz
  (15 g) butter
4 oz (115 g) sugar or honey
8 egg yolks or 5 whole eggs
brown sugar

Flavour the cream by simmering it with a vanilla pod, the sugar and a couple of bay leaves for 20 minutes. Add the strained hot cream to the whisked egg yolks and pour into ramekins.

Put the ramekins on a tray and into a low oven (110°C/225°F/Gas Mark $\frac{1}{4}$) no higher than the middle shelf for 15 minutes or so. The slower the cooking, the firmer and creamier the custard will be. The skin formed on the top of the ramekin is a good guide as to how the baking is going. Give the tray a little shake and the skin will ripple. At first it moves about in a very liquid manner, but when it is nearly cooked the skin near the edges will not move at all nor very much near the centre. Better make an extra custard if this is the first time you've baked them so that you can check if it's OK, but leave it to cool before you take a spoonful as cooking continues with the residual heat. They can be reheated if they haven't set properly. Keep in a fridge.

To make the crust, sprinkle the cold custards thickly all over with brown sugar (white sugar has an inferior taste but it will do). Place the custards in a deep tray with cold water near to the top of the ramekins and put under a fierce grill to melt the sugar and burn it a little. Don't take too long about this as the custard can spoil with too much heating. Chill until needed. The caramel will hold firm for a few hours.

Alternatively, make a caramel with sugar, 1 dessertspoon per ramekin, and just enough water to dissolve it. Boil rapidly until the bubbles become small and frothy at which point the sugar will start to take colour. Once the water has boiled away sugar browns rapidly. Pour the caramel over the chilled custards when it has cooled enough to thicken.

Or pour this caramel into the bottom of the ramekins before pouring in the uncooked custard to bake. After cooking, keep them cool for a few hours, turn the custards out of their ramekins and you have crème caramel.

Curls of orange zest, added to boiling syrup before it starts to brown, will make a caramel that is out of the ordinary. See also below (p. 146) for crystallized orange curls.

Fresh orange salad

This requires one large orange per person. Use a zester to take long curls of zest from the skin of the orange and make crystallized orange curls with them (see below). Cut the rind from the orange to leave the flesh fully exposed without a morsel of pith. With a sharp-pointed knife, slide the point into the orange along one side of a segment wall, loosening the flesh from the wall. Repeat this on the other side of the wall and continue around the orange until all the flesh is loose. Do this over a bowl to catch the juice. Prise out the flesh from the walls keeping the segments as whole as possible and discarding the pips. This is tedious until the second or third orange, by which time you'll get the hang of it. (If you can't, slice the oranges across the segments instead, it won't be as good – the pithy core is bitter and chewy – but it will do.)

Make an orange liqueur syrup using the juice from the bowl, fruit sugar and orange liqueur – fruit sugar and red wine is nice too. Pour the syrup over the oranges a few minutes before serving to let it attack the flesh a little but not more than half an hour before or it will make the firm flesh sag. Pass the candied orange curls and Amaretti biscuits around the table for guests to help themselves.

An interesting taste addition to this very 'fresh in the mouth' salad is a scattering of toasted pine kernels on the salad or passed around separately in place of the Amaretti.

Crystallized orange curls

While the peel is on the orange, attack the zest with a sharp zester, taking nice long curls from the skin (two oranges provide enough zest for six guests, but make more while you are at it – it takes no longer). Make a syrup, mixing 2

tablespoons each of sugar and water, and boil the zest in it until most of the water has evaporated. You'll see when this has happened by the size of bubbles which become smaller and finally begin to froth. This is the critical moment: from here on the syrup will start to burn. As soon as the syrup takes colour – the slightest bit of browning is enough – pour out onto a cold plate and stir around with two forks, working one against another, back to back, lifting the zest and separating it from the setting syrup. Slowly, miraculously, the sugar begins to crystallize around the zest. Continue teasing the zest until all the strands are crys-

tallized. This confection will lose its glory and turn into syrup if put onto the salad too early. It will keep for six months if stored in an airtight jar.

Ginger pudding

This dish is a fine example of what can be done with a product off the shelf. Once you have mastered the recipe – and, given the main ingredient, that is pretty easy – on no account explain to your guests how easy it is nor how clever you have been, tempting as that might be. It was extremely popular in my restaurant largely because it resisted attempts to analyse it. One or two of my regulars were particularly insistent as to how it was made and on one occasion I foolishly told one couple as they were eating it – smiles of contentment one minute became vague disappointment the next, as if they had been made a fool of. Stay mum, stay mysterious about it. One restaurant inspector declared it the third best pudding he'd ever had.

Makes 4 portions
1 ginger cake
4 oz (115 ml) whipping cream
3 oz (85 g) salted butter
1½ in (4 cm) fresh ginger
3–4 tablespoons Crabbies Ginger Wine
honey to taste

Cut the cake into 4 portions (in half horizontally then cut 2 croutes, or rounds, 3 in/8 cm

in diameter, from each slice with a pastry cutter). Fry in butter on both sides until they begin to burn. It is important that they do burn on the edges but not all over – a tricky bit of timing as one second it needs more frying and the next it is overdone: the smell will tell you when the sugar in the cake is caramelizing and that is the sign that the second has arrived.

Heat the ginger wine in a pan. Place a croute on a hot plate and pour the hot ginger wine onto it, slowly so that the wine is absorbed and doesn't ooze over the plate. Each croute will take 2–3 teaspoons of wine. Put on a spoonful of whipped cream – flavoured with grated fresh ginger and sweetened with honey – and serve immediately, before the cream slides off.

Burning the cake does two things; it adds a bitter flavour to the dish – cutting the sweetness – and it gives the cake a crust that stays a bit crunchy even though the cake itself has become trifle-soft. Any other cake will fry this way. The alcohol and cream flavourings will need adjustment accordingly.

I've had great success with Christmas pudding too – indeed this dish had its origin at one rather liquid Christmas when the pudding was forgotten until it was time to eat it. Fried in slices and served with Suzette sauce, it was the triumph of the holiday. Suzette sauce is made with equal parts of butter, sugar, orange juice and orange liqueur or brandy, all boiled together.

Chocolate soufflé

Replace the purée in the basic recipe (see p. 48) with 3–4 oz (85–115 g) of just melted, best, plain chocolate with a teaspoon of flour added to the yolks. Serve with sweetened vanilla and brandy cream.

Changing the vanilla for coffee in this cream would be good, since chocolate and coffee make a powerful combination. Use either very strong fresh coffee or best quality instant (so convenient and just as good for this purpose). On the other hand, you could stay with the vanilla in the cream and serve the soufflé with the coffee. This would be neat timing, allowing you to make the coffee while the soufflés rise. For perfection, serve with something crunchy like brandy snap, amaretti biscuit or *pain d'amandes*.

Microwaved greengages

Select firm and equally ripe greengages, remove the stems and place on a plate in the microwave, one layer deep. Microwave for 30 seconds, remove those plums that show a little froth where the stalks have been removed and give the remainder another 5–10 seconds. Repeat the process until all the greengages have frothed. Lay up on individual plates, pour over a syrup made of fruit sugar and Mirabelle eau de vie (or other plum-flavoured liqueur) and serve immediately. The vivid green skins will be plum sharp, the flesh will have a cooked plum flavour and the alcoholic syrup will accentuate the greengage taste.

7 Menu Building

Up to now, I've been dealing with those qualities in a recipe that give a dish 'good taste'. Those same qualities are the ones to make a meal memorable too. A meal is a recipe, written large and long, with a couple of extra dimensions for cooks to play with. One of those is temperature – the refreshing contrast between hot and cold food, difficult to achieve in a single dish; the other lies in the succession of dishes – allowing a cook to play down some areas of stimulation in order to increase their impact when they are finally used. One such manipulation is to avoid sweetness in a meal until the palate craves for it. How many times, after a series of stimulating savoury courses, have you felt that you just couldn't manage another mouthful of anything but somehow revive to enjoy a pudding?

So, when thinking out a menu, all those elements that make a recipe stimulating – variety in colour, texture and flavour – still need consideration but not necessarily all in one dish. For instance, if a course is predominantly green, it won't matter too much if the next is mostly green as well, since, in all probability, all the other stimulators in the second course will differ sufficiently to make it interesting without the extra stimulus of a new colour, especially if one course is hot and the other cold. Apart from ringing the changes on 'hot' and 'cold', don't forget 'warmth'. It is worth noting that the further away from blood heat the temperature of a dish, the greater is the impact of its temperature – at the extremities of temperature perception this impact is so

strong that it registers neither as hot nor cold but as pain. So, if only for the lack of temperature distraction, warm food tastes better and that alone is enough to make it equally valuable as a temperature option.

The golden rule when planning a meal is to avoid repetition. Obviously, it would be more exciting if the main ingredient in one dish differed from the next. So, for example, in an enjoyable meal fish wouldn't be followed with more fish – or only in exceptional circumstances. One could imagine what they might be: a quayside café; wriggling fish; superb variety; enthusiastic proprietor; but, even then, if this scenario was an everyday occurrence, the rule would still apply.

Happily, most main ingredients seem to me to fall into natural groups, which makes it easy to see where repetition might occur. This is my list but I imagine that anyone else attempting to group types of food – to make planning easier and menus more entertaining – would arrive at something similar.

Shellfish
Fish
Savoury eggs and cheese
Poultry and game birds (unless well hung or
  gamey)
Meat and game
Raw vegetables
Cooked vegetables
Sweet (including fresh fruit)

A well-balanced menu doesn't use the same

group twice or, if it does, not in consecutive dishes.

The easiest way of showing how to plan a meal is to give a few examples. In the menus that follow, the guiding principle has been to select dishes that give a decent contrast with each other, not just in main ingredients but in all those other elements where contrast can be effective. Recipes for the dishes selected for these menus will be found in the recipe section (to which the page number immediately following the name of the dish refers) or are contained within the menu instructions themselves.

I've orchestrated the preparation time to make the whole occasion run really smoothly, since there is nothing so distracting to the appreciation of food as a fluster in the kitchen that manages to work its way out to the dining table. It will be a comfort to know that delays between courses won't matter at all once hunger pangs stop. This happens when food passing through the mouth registers as having arrived in the stomach, and that takes about twenty minutes.

To help cooks who are working in a full-time job, I've divided the total preparation time into three: *Ahead*, which includes any preparation that can be done to food in advance of the meal – on the previous evening or in half an hour or so on the morning of the day – and that doesn't materially affect the qualities it brings to a meal; *Before the guests arrive*, which is the preparation that needs doing in the hour or so before the deadline; and *During the meal*, the work that has to be done while the meal is going on, because some ingredients can't be left hanging about. Under the heading *Variations* I have given possible substitutes for a specified dish because it may be seasonal or it may not appeal to the cook. Some effort has been made to dovetail these changes into the rest of the menu and still keep a balance of stimulants. The courses listed under these headings refer to the course recipes given in the original menu.

Menu 1

The first menu works well in providing contrasts in all departments – something worth striving for.

First course: Hot beetroot (p. 126)
Sliced, mixed with lemon juice, pepper and lots of butter. Served in ramekins, hot from the oven.

Second course: Laksa (p. 96)
A creamy Malaysian fish soup with small fish balls, fingers of chicken breast and noodles served with crisp-fried prawns – chilli hot. A substantial dish.

Third course: Savoury green salad (p. 127)
A bitter green salad with a few crisp hot slivers of meat and baby potatoes, or with cubes of toasted Feta cheese, or with garlicky croutons (a lighter option).

Fourth course: Crème brûlée (p. 144)
A baked custard with orange zest caramel.

Contrasts

Groups In each course the main ingredient falls
into a different group. In order, these groups
are cooked vegetables, fish, raw vegetables
(with flicks of meat or cheese) and sweet. There
is no repetition here, so now let's think about
tastes.

Tastes The beets are predominantly sweet and
sharp; the soup is firstly salty and then
sharp/bitter (the chilli); the salad is bitter and
salty; and the pudding is sweet with a little
bitterness (from the zest and caramel). Notice
how the sweetness is almost totally absent from
the middle courses – the practice I talked of
earlier.

Colours Deep red beets make a nice contrast
to the creamy soup, which is white/beige with
flecks of red. The green salad is good followed
by the brown/orange pudding. Colour contrasting is a bit of a finesse since dishes don't
appear all together, but it is a good habit to
get into. To have the same colour – say red –
in all courses would be boring visually.

Textures Clearly warm and slightly chewy
beets with a butter succulence make a nice
contrast to the creamy slurpy soup. Then a
crisp salad with soft cooked potatoes is followed by the smooth custard. French bread

with a really crunchy crust will be good served
with the beets or the salad.

Temperature Warm beets are followed by hot
soup, a cool salad and a cold sweet.

Timing

Ahead

First course The beetroot starter can be made
completely and left in the fridge, ready to be
warmed up. Clingfilm the ramekins to stop the
top layer of beets drying out.
Second course Prepare the soup base: make
the fish balls and freeze; lightly marinate the
sliced raw chicken in grated fresh ginger and
salty lemon juice and keep in the fridge; pre-
cook the noodles and chill.
Third course Make the vinaigrette. If the meat
and potatoes variation is chosen, boil the
potatoes and chill, and slice and marinate the
raw meat and keep cold. If the Feta cheese is
chosen, dress the cheese with oil and paprika
and grill on both sides; when cold, cut into
cubes but leave in the dish with the oil. If
croutons are chosen, toast the bread well and
shallow-dip into browned garlic oil; they will
need a reheat in the oven just before serving,
since the crunch factor is super-critical.
Fourth course Make custards completely.
Keep cold and clingfilmed.

Before the guests arrive

Heat the oven to warm (160°C/325°F/Gas Mark 3).

First course   Heat the beets in their ramekins in the oven about half an hour before the meal starts. Crisp up the bread crust in the oven for ten minutes.

Second course   Warm up the soup slowly, just before sitting down for the first course. Heat garlic oil and butter in pan and fry the prawns a bit; put to one side. Defrost the fish balls. Chop the coriander (stalks and all), spring onions and water chestnuts to a size that will fit comfortably onto a soup spoon.

Third course   Part-fry the potatoes and meats in garlic oil. Wash the greens for the salad and break into bite-sized pieces; leave in a colander or salad spinner in a cool place.

Fourth course   Remove custards from fridge.

During the meal

First course   Serve the beets with crusty warm bread.

Second course   Bring the soup to a simmer, add the fish balls and raw chicken. Fry off the prawns until they are a bit smaller and are beginning to get chewy, then put them in a serving dish. Check that the fish balls and chicken are cooked by tasting them; add pre-cooked noodles, water-chestnuts, spring onions, a little more fresh, grated ginger and coriander to the soup, and remove from the heat. Serve the soup in bowls and pass around the prawn sambal for guests to spoon over the soup, warning them that it is hot.

Third course   Finish frying the meat and baby unpeeled potatoes to get crisp edges and skins; or reheat the Feta cheese or croutons in the oven. Meanwhile dry the salad and put it onto the vinaigrette already in the salad bowl. Add the meat and potato (or cheese or croutons) and toss at the table.

Fourth course   Unwrap the custards and serve.

Variations

First course   If beets are out of season (after Christmas they are pale and woody), or you don't care for them, you could substitute garlicky mushrooms (p. 126). Nothing would change in the contrasts except exchanging rich red for darkest brown/black, which still makes a nice contrast to the white soup.

Second course   A less last-minute course would be goulashsuppe (p. 100) where small bits of meat and vegetables in a rich mahogany soup are brightened with a dollop of really sharp sour cream. Make a cucumber, coriander and fresh chilli relish to pass around for colour and table interest, ie keeping the conversation on the food.

Third course   If you've decided on goulashsuppe, clearly the meat and potatoes option for the salad would be out, as you don't want two meat courses side by side.

Fourth course   A rich little chocolate pot would be great instead of the custard but not after that substantial goulashsuppe – better then to make the lighter Amber's chocolate pudding or a fresh orange salad.

Menu 2

A five-course menu, but not too filling.

First course: Grilled mussels (p. 108)
Mussels in a drop of their own juice on their half-shells, with a grilled topping.

Second course: Cream of parsnip soup (p. 98)
With sour tamarind and toasted cumin, dressed with paprika.

Third course: Hot chicken salad (p. 116)
With green beans and coriander.

Fourth course: Pot of toasted cheese (p. 105)
With grissini (the thin rusk sticks from Italy) and sliced gherkins if you like them.

Fifth course: Fresh orange salad (p. 145)
With candied orange zest and served with something crunchy like an almond biscuit, brandysnap or Amaretti.

Contrasts

Groups Shellfish, cooked vegetables, poultry and nearly raw vegetables, cheese, sweet.

Tastes Salty mussels and bitter toasted cheese are followed by the sour and slightly sweet parsnip soup with its bitter toasted cumin. Then comes the salty, sour and sweet chicken salad, followed by the salty bitterness and lactic acid sourness of the cheese, all of which is rounded off nicely by the sweet and sour orange salad. The saltiness of the savoury dishes is made palatable by being married to a different second flavour in each course.

Colours Orange and brown mussels in their dramatic blue/purple shells contrast well with the cream soup with its red paprika streak. This is followed by the green and pale brown salad; the brown and cream cheese and the orange salad.

Textures The chewy mussels contrast with the slurpy soup, while the crisp and chewy salad is followed by the soft spoonable cheese with the crunchy grissini. Next is the slurpy fruit salad with its chewy zest and crunchy biscuit.

Temperature Warm mussels, hot soup and the warm-to-hot chicken work well with the warm cheese and cold salad.

Timing

Ahead

First course   Cook the mussels and leave on a half shell in juice in the fridge. Make freshbreadcrumb and Parmesan topping.

Second course   Make the soup and toast the
cumin (although it is quite a good idea to do
this just before the meal, as the aroma then is
very appetite arousing).

Third course   Make the dressing. Fry off the
almonds and keep airtight. On the day (in the
morning perhaps) marinate the chicken.

Fourth course   Make the rarebit mix and pot
up in ramekins.

Fifth course   Do absolutely nothing to the fruit
part of the salad – freshness is all – but make
an orange liqueur syrup, not too sweet, and
remove the zest from the oranges in long curls
with a zester and candy them. Put into an airtight jar.

Before the guests arrive

First course   Assemble the mussels and prop
them level in the grill pan. Get the grill started
so as to be hot and quick when the guests are
seated; you could grill the mussels now and
keep them warm, but you risk drying them out.

Second course   Heat the soup, but don't boil it.

Third course   Blanch and refresh the beans,
chop the coriander and part-fry the chicken.

Fourth course   Turn the oven onto a moderate
180°C/350°F/Gas Mark 4.

Fifth course   Peel oranges with a knife, removing all white pith so that the flesh is completely
exposed. Slice thinly across the segments or,
better, remove flesh from between the
segment walls.

During the meal

First course   Serve the mussels on one large
plate in the centre of the table.

Second course   Pour or ladle the soup into *hot*
bowls and decorate them in the kitchen. Finish
frying chicken after the first course and put it
into the moderate oven together with the
cheese pots. Put fruit segments into liqueur
syrup.

Third course   Stir-fry beans and coriander,
slice chicken breasts and lay these onto the
beans, add dressing and top with fried almonds.

Fourth course   Grill cheese brown before
serving.

Fifth course   Serve salad and sprinkle with
candied zest just before serving.

Variations

First course   Try stir-fried king prawns (p. 109)
instead of mussels. This is another hot, fishy
finger food – less work in advance but more at
the end. A cold starter would do nicely: prosciutto with sweet fruit or maybe smoked
salmon with sour cream and blinis.

Second course   Any other creamy vegetable
soup or the light and unusual Bramley mulligatawny soup (p. 79) would be a replacement
here. Gazpacho (p. 101) would be nice in
summer since the starter is hot.

Third course   Use veal escalopes or pork
instead of chicken, mangetout or broccoli
instead of beans, and any other fresh herb
(dill, etc.).

Fourth course A cheese board or a mature Cheddar with a well-flavoured apple (Cox's Orange or a Russet) here would allow time for making the following alternative sweet.
Fifth course Delicious lemon pudding: a bit last minute but more spectacular. See p. 49.

In the following menus, each course is contrasted in the same way as the menus above but how that contrast works I leave to your imagination. I've still given the timing since it may not be obvious what will spoil if kept overnight.

Menu 3

First course: Gazpacho (p. 101)

Second course: Two-way duck (p. 115)
With Seville oranges and spinach-wrapped rice.

Third course: Tomato and sweet white onion salad

Fourth course: Ginger pudding (p. 146)

Timing

Ahead

First course Nothing here can be done in advance, for fear of losing the green colour.
Second course Make two-way duck stew flavoured with oranges; freeze the raw breasts.

Blanch leaf spinach and use it to line individual buttered ramekins leaving enough leaf outside to fold over the filling. Pack the ramekins with boiled rice, flavoured with four-spice powder, and fold the spinach over the rice to make neat green parcels. Leave the ramekins in the fridge.
Third course Nothing here can be done in advance.
Fourth course Cut cake into round croûtes, wrap and chill.

Before the guests arrive

Heat oven to moderate (180°C/350°F/Gas Mark 4).
First course Make gazpacho and chill; if you've time, toast a few pine kernels to sprinkle onto it.
Second course Take breasts from freezer, score the skin through with close cuts and rub salt into those cuts. Grill the skins brown and crisp, then heat them in the bottom of the oven – slowly. Reheat rice ramekins in the oven now or microwave them later. Gently reheat duck stew.
Third course Slice tomatoes and onions thinly. Keep them separate and sprinkle both with salt and the onions with a splash of wine vinegar. Later, lay them out prettily in a plate and dress with vinaigrette.
Fourth course Grate fresh ginger and mix with honey.

During the meal

First course Serve the gazpacho and pass

round the toasted pine kernels, if you have them, or otherwise crisp, crusty bread.

Second course Check the breasts to see if they are cooked enough: they should be fairly elastic when pressed. If in doubt cut one in half to see and, if it is raw, either fry the breasts flesh-side down until just beginning to brown or put them in the top of the oven. Heat the stew while the soup is drunk.

Turn out the ramekins directly onto the plates, surround with duck stew and lay slices of the breasts on top (cut thinly, across the grain); each slice should be nicely pink with its own bit of crisp skin. The slicing is not at all difficult with a sharp knife.

Third course Before the duck course is finished, pass round the tomato salad to eat off the same plate; the gravy accents it nicely.

Fourth course Whip the cream and flavour with ginger honey. Fry the croutes, put them on plates and dress with hot ginger wine and a dollop of cream.

Variations

First course The charred peppers that feature in the next menu would do nicely here, too.

Second course The two-way method used with the duck works superbly well with guineafowl, pheasant or other game birds, since it allows the tougher meat to be stewed tender without overcooking (and drying out) the breasts – the best of both worlds really. Compensate for the lack of crispy duck skin with equally crisp, grilled streaky bacon.

Third course A green herb salad would be nice here but for the colour of the spinach wrapping – which, however, may not be an important consideration for you. When using game birds for the second course, move the citrus element of the stew into a watercress, celeriac and orange segment salad.

Fourth course Almost any sweet and not too sharp pudding would do here. It would need a little succulence: home-made icecream with a splash of sweet liqueur would go down well, as would a little pot of chocolate (p. 144).

Menu 4

First course: Charred red peppers (p. 129)
With anchovies.

Second course: A cup of clear borsch (p. 101)
With toasted garlic croutons (p. 142) in the saucer.

Third course: Fried cutlets of salmon with fresh pesto (p. 137)
Accompanied by warm potato and broccoli with a browned garlic vinaigrette (p. 132).

Fourth course: Peaches in red wine

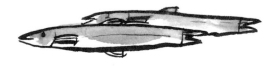

Timing

Ahead

First course   Char the peppers and dress generously with olive oil.
Second course   Make borsch.
Third course   Make browned garlic vinaigrette.
Fourth course   Make a red wine syrup using fruit sugar and claret for preference.

Before the guests arrive

Heat oven to moderate (180°C/350°F/Gas Mark 4).
First course   Lay peppers with anchovies, and sprinkle with pepper (bright pepper is particularly good here if you have it made) and a squeeze of lemon.
Second course   Make garlic croutons and keep them warm in the bottom of the oven.
Third course   Fry one side of each salmon cutlet brown, cook the potatoes and blanch the broccoli. Assemble pesto ingredients in blender.
Fourth course   Peel peaches and cover with cold water, to which some lemon juice has been added, providing an acid to stop the peaches going brown.

During the meal

First course   Serve.
Second course   Heat the soup, but don't boil it, as boiling ruins the colour. Also heat the croutons in the oven. Serve the soup in the cup, and the croutons in the saucer.
Third course   Put the salmon into the middle of the oven. Heat a saucepan of water, ready to reheat the vegetables, or put them with a drop of water in a flat dish, clingfilm covered, for reheating in the microwave. If no microwave, put vegetables in the boiling water for two to three minutes, drain and dress with vinaigrette. Serve the salmon, brown side up on a pool of pesto, with vegetables.
Fourth course   Slice peaches, add the red wine syrup and warm the combination in the microwave, or put the peaches into the hot syrup before sitting down to the salmon. They should be warm and slightly affected by the red syrup but by no means cooked.

Variations

First course   Another cold starter like salami with gherkins or prosciutto with ripe figs or melon would be nice here.
Second course   Borsch is both rich and light. Provided that you stick with the charred peppers, a clear chicken or beef consommé with a fresh herb element would work well, as would Bramley mulligatawny soup (p. 79).
Third course   Any rich fried fish like mackerel, or even fillets of herring with a tart sauce (puréed gooseberries with an anise-flavoured herb like fennel or tarragon, for instance), would be good but exchange the first two courses for a chicory, watercress, Gruyère and walnut salad.
Fourth course   A fruity freshness is what the

peaches supply, so almost any fruit/alcohol combination would be enjoyable here as long as it's not too rich. I'd leave out any thought of cream.

Menu 5

First course: Lentil and tamarind soup (p. 99)

Second course: Escabèche (p. 113)

Third course: Hot chicken and bean salad (p. 116)

Fourth course: Delicious lemon pudding (p. 49)

This menu is comparatively hassle-free when the time comes for it to be served. By the time the soup is hot, the escabèche is ready to follow and all that needs doing then is a bit of stir-frying and whipping the egg-whites for the pudding. Either of the first two courses can be left out for a lighter meal.

Timing

Ahead

First course   Make the soup and toast the cumin seed (to be sprinkled on the soup before serving).
Second course   Fry the fish – firm, white fillets of cod for instance – until one side is nicely brown; depending on the thickness of the fish, that may be all the frying it needs. Lay the fish, brown side up on a bed of thinly sliced, sweet onions or spring onions in a well-fitting dish. Make enough vinaigrette to just cover the fish, but replace half the usual amount of oil with white wine; heat it and pour onto the fish. The heating is to speed the softening of the onions and is unnecessary if this dish is to be left overnight.
Third course   Marinate the chicken breasts; trim and blanch the beans very lightly; cook the noodles and rinse until cold. Reserve beans and noodles under cover in the fridge. Fry almonds and toss them in four-spice powder (p. 167) and salt; put them into a screw-top jar.
Fourth course   Make up the pudding recipe, leaving only the whipping and folding in of the egg-whites to be done.

Before the guests arrive

Heat the oven to 200°C/400°F/Gas Mark 6.
First course   Heat the soup.
Second course   If you want to serve the escabèche warm, put it into an ovenproof dish and heat it in the oven before the soup is served. Lay the fish on a serving dish; pour over it the vinaigrette with onions; sprinkle on some fresh-chopped herb.
Third course   Fry the chicken breasts nicely brown on one side, lightly brown on the other and put into the bottom of the oven.

During the meal

First course Serve.
Second course Serve.
Third course Stir-fry the beans and add the noodles and the marinade from the chicken breasts. Cut up the chicken breasts and fold them into the beans and noodles, then sprinkle with almonds.
Fourth course Whip the egg-whites to a soft peak and fold them into the pudding; pour into ramekins and pop into the oven on a medium-to-high shelf for 10–15 minutes.

Variations

This menu might well be improved by serving the fish first. It would allow for the soup to be heated while the fish is being served, but it would bring the two hot dishes together.
First course To keep the ingredient balance any vegetable soup would be fine – a home-made tomato soup, for instance.
Second course I enjoy a little fresh chilli in the vinaigrette. Other than that, soused mackerel is the nearest substitute but cold, poached, smoked haddock or a boned kipper treated as above is good too.
Third course Roast slices of belly pork (put in a medium oven, dressed with fresh ginger/soy/honey marinade, sprinkled with four-spice powder and cooked until both sides are nicely browned) are a favourite of mine and cut into suitable chunks would substitute very well for the chicken here. Change the almonds for walnuts if you do this.
Fourth course Delicious lemon pudding is hard to beat as it looks so special and gives the whole menu a bit of class, but ginger pudding would fit well with the preceding chicken although it would be a bit rich to follow belly pork. Perhaps the humble apple crumble, given a lift by spicing the crumble with ground coriander, cardamom and mace and using honey or brown sugar instead of granulated sugar (lemon or orange zest or calvados in the apple is good too), is both intense and refreshing and, perhaps more to the point, can be made well ahead; just keep the crumble off the cooked apple until it is ready to be put in the oven, when the chicken course is served.

8 Timesavers and Shortcuts

During the making of the average meal, the pace of preparation starts at a steady unhurried trot and rises to a gallop, as all the components fight for time to be spent on them just before the meal begins. Even if the meal has been planned carefully so that at least some dishes need no last-minute attention (these are the ones that wait around patiently without changing their nature), the others, with less tolerant manners, will quicken the pace at the crucial time. Any sleight of hand that helps to relieve this congestion without reducing the quality must be good news.

In the previous chapter, which dealt with assembling a meal from complementary dishes, there are examples of the way a thoughtful cook can prepare parts of these dishes ahead of time without the quality suffering. This chapter focuses on these advance preparations.

Freezing

A big ally in getting ahead, this method of preservation leaves the flavour of most foods intact even if it is not so hot at preserving its texture – at least this is true of uncooked foods. Cooked food has had its nature (including texture) changed by heat already and comes from the freezer practically indistinguishable from its pre-frozen state.

It is worth pointing out that food deteriorates in a freezer just as it does in a fridge or on a cold shelf in a pantry but at a much slower rate: what will keep for three days in the fridge will keep, as fresh, in a freezer for a month.

While it takes forever to defrost a large lump, small pieces are quickly brought back to life. So, when freezing food, prepare and freeze it in small pieces and, when freezing liquid, freeze it in cubes – ice cube trays are fine for this – which can be bagged together for storage so that you are able to take from the freezer just the amount you need and no more. Not only does it save time in defrosting but it keeps the unused amounts in a healthier condition than if they have to be refrozen. Refreezing is dangerous if the food has completely thawed out and become warm enough for microbe development.

Cooked Timesavers From the Freezer

Stocks

When making a stock for a dish, make more than you will need. Reduce the surplus to a glaze to concentrate the flavour and then freeze into cubes. Store these in the freezer, well bagged and clearly marked, for use in penny pinches as needed. So often, all a sauce needs is the glutinous mouth effect of stock to round off its appeal and it is very handy to reach into the freezer rather than make stock especially each time you need it.

As a restaurateur, I kept several kinds of stock cubes in my freezer but, for home cooks, it is quite enough to have three: fish, chicken and one made from browned meat bones. These will cover most eventualities. For recipes see pp. 94–5.

If you don't happen to have meat stock cubes in your freezer you can use condensed beef consommé from a can instead. And if, lacking the appropriate, frozen stock cube, you have to fall back on packaged dried stock cubes, remember that the largest difference in the mouth between these and frozen stock is the lack of the above-mentioned, glutinous mouth effect. This can be supplied by adding gelatine: allow $\frac{1}{2}$ oz (15 g) of gelatine for every dried stock cube used. Neither are as good as honest stock but they do an adequate job of stimulation in a slightly different way and few guests are going to notice the difference.

Sauces

Béchamel is a non-specific, general-purpose white sauce (see p. 130). Make it without seasoning (so that the cubes can be used with sweet or savoury dishes), cook it long enough to get rid of its floury taste and freeze into cubes. Reach for a béchamel cube when a thin sauce you are adjusting needs a smooth, creamy whiteness and needs it really quickly. The smaller the cubes, the quicker this this can be. The biggest hazard of making egg custard, overheating (which makes it separate), can be lessened if a béchamel cube has been added before thickening begins.

Duxelles sauce is made from sweated mushrooms and shallots and is very useful as a good flavourful base to savoury sauces, especially for vegetarian dishes. It follows that to have some in cube form in the freezer is a good backstop if unannounced vegetarians call. See p. 131.

Seasoned butters

Melted butter is used as a dressing to add succulence to vegetables but is rarely thought of as a dressing for anything else these days. Think again, though, and it becomes a ready-made, convenient, uncooked sauce whenever there is a need for juice in a dish. Seasoned butters have a rare brightness for all their simplicity. The standard method is to place portions of seasoned butter, shaped as thin medallions, on hot food to melt as it is being served. Cutting butter into neat medallions requires it to be refrigerator-cold but not frozen. Fashion cool, seasoned butter into a long cylinder, about $1\frac{1}{2}$ in (4 cm) in diameter, and chill. Slice into $\frac{1}{4}$ in (6 mm) thick roundels and then freeze them, not touching. Bag and label later. See pp. 139–140 for savoury and sweet butters.

Pancakes

Make pancakes at leisure (see p. 102) and let them cool. Layer each with clingfilm and freeze in a pile. They keep, frozen, for 2–3 months. Reheat them, straight from the freezer, by frying one side only. To fry both sides is to run the risk of the pancakes drying out. Having frozen pancakes makes the production of an impressive dish like crêpes Suzette a matter of minutes (see p. 147 for Suzette Sauce).

Several sorts of pancake can be made from one batter: add grated lemon zest and a little sugar to the batter and use the resulting pancakes for rolling round sweet apple purée to make apple turnovers; or, changing lemon zest for orange, use the batter to make Polish pancakes (see p. 103).

A good handful of chopped herb – parsley or mint or dill – will speckle the batter green and set off a red sauce or filling very nicely. Conversely a pancake reddened by adding a spoon of tomato purée or paprika to the batter makes a contrasting wrapping around a green filling like spinach with curd cheese.

Frozen sliced bread

Keeping bread in a freezer stops it deteriorating as fast as it would in a fridge and having it sliced means that it is available, slice by slice, for frying or toasting. The frozen interior gives the chance for the surface to brown without drying out the inside which stays steamily moist. Keeps for 2–3 months.

Uncooked Timesavers From the Freezer

Fricadelles

These spicy pork balls have a long freezer life. Grape-sized fricadelles will turn soup, or pasta, from a starter into a main course and small ones can be used straight from the freezer. Ones made the size of golf balls, which take a little longer in the oven from frozen, are perfect for a cheap main course and are sufficiently unusual to avoid odious comparison with rissoles. These are a really useful, economic standby. See p. 114.

Raw fish balls

These are made with raw white fish, blended in a processor, seasoned, fashioned into small, grape-sized balls and rolled in rice flour. Make them ahead of the time you need them as they can be frozen, uncooked, without hurt. They are good straight from the freezer, in fishy soups like laksa, in a fishy sauce with pasta or noodles or fried and sprinkled with lemon juice as a canapé. See p. 97 for a recipe.

Mushrooms

These freeze perfectly but soften as they thaw so they can't be used as you would uncooked ones. However, in their softened state, they are perfect for garlicky mushrooms (see p. 126). Buy mushrooms by the box when the price is right. Trim the stalks to the level of the mushroom cup edge and freeze, not touching, on a tray, then bag. I love the open dark brown gilled ones as they have so much more flavour. Use the stalk trimmings to make mushroom relish (see p. 136).

Fresh herbs

When herbs are plentiful, they can be frozen – not for decoration, since they lose colour and become floppy, but for flavour.

Other Timesavers

Garlic oil

This paragon, on which I have rhapsodized earlier, adds a depth to savoury cooking that nothing else seems to match. As with so many recipes, making a quantity is almost as easy as making a little, and having it available constantly is sheer luxury. Rarely, in the kitchen, can so little time be used to better effect.

If you intend using garlic oil uncooked, it needs to be freshly made, but if it is to be used for cooking, it keeps sweet and ungarlicky (in the worst 'phew, garlic' sense) in a fridge for 3 or 4 days.

½ pint (285 ml) cooking oil
5–6 large cloves of garlic, peeled and roughly chopped

Put both ingredients into a blender bowl (or a deep and narrow container, if you have a hand-held blender). Blend until the garlic and oil have turned into a milky purée.

Uses

I use it mostly instead of plain oil for frying savoury foods. Heat the garlic oil gently, allowing it to brown in the pan before introducing whatever you had in mind to fry. Any trace of garlic smell evaporates and you are left with a sweet, nutty brown oil with a rich flavour and an even richer aroma, seductive enough to be almost addictive but hardly garlicky. This richness will give an underpinning to the flavour of any food fortunate enough to be fried in it. The minuscule bits of garlic in the oil brown and stick to food very prettily.

Use it instead of plain oil at the start of making sauces for pasta. Browning a fresh chopped chilli in garlic oil and adding a squeeze of lemon, a few curls of zest and a handful of fresh herb is the easiest way to paradise in pasta that I know. It is better still if you have used olive oil in the blending.

Garlic oil is splendid browned with butter as a noisette to dress boiled vegetables or fish. To produce browned garlic oil, fry it gently until the garlic bits are light brown (beige might be a better description) and use it to make a vinaigrette or a mayonnaise with a wonderfully nutty top note.

Paint it on roasts and grills before cooking. Do this and there will be no need to spike the roasts with slivers of garlic.

Add just a drop or two to gravies at the last moment. Dribble it on the fresh-breadcrumb topping of grilled oysters, lasagne or other breadcrumbed dishes before the final browning. And, of course, it is splendid for garlic croutons (see p. 142).

Variation

This method of blending flavour into oil need not be restricted to garlic. I've had wonderful results from blending small amounts of fresh chilli into plain or garlic oil. It is a simple way of diluting the heat of chilli into a bright liveliness. All fresh herbs can be blended; try dark green dill oil with gravadlax – it is magical.

Condiments For the Kitchen Shelf

Make these and you will be able to inject most bland dishes with a touch of instant brilliance. Part of their dazzle is the novel taste they have, and there is no doubt that constantly repeating the same formula reduces their impact – certainly to the cook who makes them. Change the formula after making a batch or two.

Chilli vinegar and oil

This is nice to have on the shelf when fresh chilli isn't to hand. Put a heaped teaspoon of small dried chillies into half a pint (285 ml) of vinegar, salty enough to prick the tongue, then add about half as much sugar as salt. Leave for a month and it should be hot enough for you never to buy Tabasco again. Keep in a cool place.

Chilli oil is even more simple: just substitute oil for the salted vinegar, keep in a warm place and wait for a month. Chillies have enough bite to flavour several batches of oil.

Mixed spice powders

These blends of spices can be ground way ahead and not lose their sparkle or originality. Sprinkle them on low-profile food, like a fairy sprinkling of magic dust, to transform them at the last minute. I even carry the first one I made with me every time I take a plane. All that blandness in little plastic trays made me despair of ever enjoying airline food until I discovered dukkah.

Dukkah

The formula for this North African toasted spice powder varies with every maker. Use it as an exotic top note to make predictable food more unusual and more exciting.

2 parts sesame seed
1 part coriander seed
1 part cumin seed
1 part hazelnuts
salt and pepper to taste

Toast and grind each ingredient separately since they brown and grind at different rates. I use a coffee grinder for the grinding and, with nuts particularly, it is easy to over-grind and finish with a paste rather than a free-flowing powder. Hazelnuts should be broken up small before grinding to make this less likely. Mix the powdered ingredients together and test a portion with salt and fresh ground pepper, adding a little at a time until the taste of it pleases. For maximum effect, serve it as a table condiment – don't cook with it. This mix is so good that it makes bread, dipped in it, interesting enough to eat on its own. This, I'm told, is the Arab way at breakfast time.

Bright pepper

3 parts, by weight, black peppercorns
2 parts, by weight, dried green peppercorns
1 part Szechuan pepper
1 part blade mace

Grind and mix together for a wildly aromatic powder that makes a pepper mill an unnecessary accessory. This pepper can be used during or after cooking.

Four-spice powder

Five-spice powder is more usual but I'm not partial to anise flavours and leave out star anise, one of the traditional five.

1 part Szechuan pepper
1 part cassia bark (or cinnamon – an inferior
  substitute)
1 part fennel seed
1 part cloves
½ parts of salt and sugar

Grind each ingredient separately and mix together and keep in an airtight jar.

This will be immediately recognizable as the background flavour underpinning quite a number of Chinese dishes. It still has a smack of anise about it from the fennel seed and Szechuan pepper. Some people include an equal part of dried orange peel in the mix too. It is complementary but I prefer to add fresh orange zest instead. If you must have five-spice powder, add a half part of whole star anise (ground of course) or, if you have my problem, you could try celery seed. The mixture matures with a week or two's keeping. This is a cooking powder so sprinkle it on food before grilling or frying to develop its full richness.

Garam masala

This mainstay of Indian cooking is readily found, dull and flaccid, in most food shops. Use this stale stuff if you must, but know that, although the taste of the ready-made will give a 'spicy' background, the power and brilliance of the freshly ground powder is in another street altogether. This is cooking powder.

1 oz (30 g) black peppercorns
1 oz (30 g) coriander seed
1 oz (30 g) caraway or cumin seed
10 pods of cardamoms, seeds only
½ oz (15 g) cassia bark
¼ oz (7 g) cloves

Grind each separately then mix together. Keep the mixture cool, dark and airtight and use within 3 months or start again. Toast the coriander and cumin for an even more vivid flavour but a much shorter shelf life.

Shortcuts Off the Shelf

Twenty years ago I was dining in a smart Home Counties restaurant when the proprietor came to my table to ask how I was enjoying the meal. We had roast lamb with haricot beans as the main course and I said how delicious and perfectly cooked the haricots were. He thanked me for the compliment and left the table with a smile. Later, when I went to his desk to pay the bill, he came close to me and quietly said that he was pleased I had enjoyed his haricots and if I wanted to make them myself it was easy, since they were only baked beans – with every hint of sauce rinsed away – served with garlic browned in lamb fat, a squeeze of lemon and a load of parsley. I left with mixed emotions; pleased to have found such an easy way of making haricots (and they had been very good, even in retrospect) and pleased that the proprietor had told me his nifty shortcut, yet somehow feeling foolish at being taken in. I should have guessed, because haricots don't look the same as the navy beans used in commercial baked beans.

This object lesson has made me extremely careful, almost enigmatic, when I'm complimented after using ready-made goods (like baked beans) undetected. I never confess (although the urge to do so is almost irresistible at times), since I risk making them feel as foolish as I had all that time ago.

If a shortcut is detected, it only shows that you aren't as good a cook as you thought. Don't feel bad about it. Using cooking skills on ready-made goods is just as creative as using them on basic ingredients and most manufactured products are so bland that they cry out for creative improvement. Most of the ways I use to zip up a sauce or a salad work equally well on them. See pp. 70–71.

Whenever I feel the need for something new to work on and I can't find it at the greengrocer or the butcher, I take a ramble around a supermarket looking for new products. Often the look of the packaging promises more than the contents within, so it is prudent to look at the ingredients list. There, the constituents are listed in order of quantity, so you can get a fair idea of how the dish will taste before buying. Something can be done to all of them, since they are light on freshness by their very nature and very probably short on crisp or crunchy textures, too. Once the shortcoming has been identified, it is often very simple to put it right. The following list of good, old stand-bys is usually to be found on my shelves.

Canned Goods

Cooked beans Apart from the almost too-well-known baked beans in tomato sauce, most of the varieties are in plain liquids and need working on anyway. There are some fairly bland Indian pulse concoctions on the market begging to be transformed with a small amount of chopped ready-made Indian pickles and browned garlic oil.

Tinned tomatoes These are splendid substitutes for cooked fresh tomatoes, especially if a little acidity is added. For a really rich sauce, strain them and reduce the liquid with butter and a little pepper before returning the tomato solids.

Condensed tomato purée There was a time when the use of this used to shout from the plate, but nowadays the quality is excellent – the condensing less. It is a brilliant shortcut to boiling, skinning, deseeding and reducing fresh tomatoes. Today 'sun-dried tomatoes' are fashionable (the flavour of which rather reminds me of the old-fashioned, condensed tomato purée) and handy to slice into salads or to be served in their oil as an authentic Italian antipasto. Use the oil as a dressing for pasta.

Asparagus Strain off the liquid and reduce it with half a packet chicken-stock cube, before adding it, with the chopped asparagus, to cooked peas and rice, bolstered with some grated Parmesan. This makes an interesting variation to the well-known Venetian speciality *risi e bisi* (rice cooked in veal stock with peas and herbs).

Corned beef Slice the corned beef and fry it, gently at first, in garlic oil with fine chopped chilli or paprika. Once the slices have slackened, turn up the heat and shred the beef. Fry the shreds until crisp. Use these as a meaty topping on the above mentioned *risi e bisi* to turn it from a starter to a main course. If you put them on soft fried noodles, as part of a Chinese meal, add four-spice powder to the frying oil. It is vital that the shreds are kept crisp since that is their biggest charm.

Condiments

When I started cooking, ready-made condiments seemed sent from God. It took time to realize that these concoctions provided, along with the taste I used them for, a lot of other baggage that I preferred not to have – not the least of which was their readily identifiable flavours. Now I know more about isolating what a dish needs by way of attracting attention, I use less of these portmanteau products and with more moderation. If you can identify it, you've used too much.

Worcestershire sauce This has flavours of the tart and fruity tamarind, of chilli and of malt vinegar. Where all of these are needed or the dish can stand them, I still use it, but tamarind purée, fresh chilli and wine vinegar are better if they are to hand. Used moderately, Worcestershire sauce 'disappears' and it seems indispensable in stewed cheese (see p. 105) or Welsh rarebit.

Tabasco This well-known spiker of tomato juice is hot but is not as bright as fresh chilli. It's handy if you haven't made your own chilli vinegar (see p. 166).

Bottled mint sauce It comes condensed, needing vinegar, and is no substitute for fresh-made mint sauce, but it is as good as frozen mint and better than dried mint for brightness. It has a slight chemical/saccharine taste that stops me using it a lot more. If there are no fresh herbs around, I reach for it.

French mustard There is a twang to ready-made English mustard that seems redolent of burger houses. This association stops me enjoying it as a taste in its own right, and the same could be said for French mustard, but my links with it are more historic. I find it perfectly acceptable used as part of a vinaigrette or as part of a coating for meats to be grilled.

Mango, lime or aubergine pickle These off-the-shelf Indian pickles are so vivid compared to packaged curry powders. Use them, well chopped up, in rice, yoghurt, or lentils for a home-made Indian taste. They are acidic, but that is part of why I like them anyway. Steer clear of garlic pickle which has a stale taste that stays on the breath.

Oyster sauce This Chinese sauce is quite delicious, meatily savoury and not that strong on oyster taste. It is great with steaks and other grilled meats. A very popular use is with stir-fried greens and toasted almonds. Buy the best, YKY (Yu Kwen Yick), if available, but the others, tasting a little like HP sauce, are better than nothing.

Black bean sauce This is another popular Chinese condiment, which I stir into fried rice. The small fermented beans are easily overlooked in a spoonful of rice and create quite an interest when bitten on.

Peanut butter Used sparingly, this tastes of toasted nuts not peanuts. Dissolve it into the oil to be used for frying rice or couscous for a good, non-specific nutty taste. Crunchy peanut butter will be specific, the small bits of peanut give the game away, so use the smooth.

Balachan An East Indies seasoning made from rotted prawns or shrimps compressed into a block. It is pungent and off-putting on its own but can be used as an underpinning to other strong flavours with magical effect. Chips grated off the solid block can be fried in oil long enough for them to dissolve into a purée.

Keep it in an air-tight container. Since frying it is a smelly business and not one to be repeated too often, brace yourself and fry a quantity on a windy day, or fry it out of doors, for the resultant flavour is so oriental that it can make any Far Eastern meal seem really authentic. I used to keep it as a stand-by for oriental evenings but now I find it creeping into more everyday cooking in place of tinned anchovies. A little goes a very long but good way to intensify a rich *umami* taste. In a cool place the purée will keep for six months at least.

Creamed coconut This is a fair imitation of fresh coconut, close enough to stop me buying fresh nuts when a recipe calls for it. What it lacks is texture, which in this particular case I'm pleased about. Eating coconut flesh demands a toothpick afterwards. It comes in a block but there are individual packets of powder, too.

Bamboo shoots and water chestnuts Although these aren't a patch on the fresh originals, the tinned versions do keep their crunch factor, even when cooked, and are useful where that alone is needed.

Index

Page numbers in **bold** refer to recipes.